Isaac Penington

## Letters of Issac Penington

An Eminent Minister of the Gospel in the Society of Friends

Isaac Penington

**Letters of Issac Penington**
*An Eminent Minister of the Gospel in the Society of Friends*

ISBN/EAN: 9783337021986

Printed in Europe, USA, Canada, Australia, Japan

Cover: Foto ©ninafisch / pixelio.de

More available books at **www.hansebooks.com**

# LETTERS

## OF

## ISAAC PENINGTON,

## AN EMINENT MINISTER OF THE GOSPEL

### IN

### The Society of Friends.

---

"He hath filled the hungry with good things; and the rich he hath sent empty away."—Luke i. 53.

---

PHILADELPHIA:
PUBLISHED BY THE
BOOK ASSOCIATION OF FRIENDS.
1879.

# PREFACE.

The following letters form part of a collection published by John Barclay in England in 1828, and since republished in this country. Their author, Isaac Penington, was a member and minister of the religious society of Friends, and was the son of Alderman Penington, of London, who during two years was Mayor of that city, and a noted member of the Long Parliament. The letters were written at various intervals between the time at which Isaac Penington joined the Society of Friends, which was about the year 1658, and his death, which took place in 1679.

Both the English and American editions having been exhausted, it has been thought that it might be useful to reprint such of the letters as could be comprised in a volume of this series. With reference to economy of space, the selection is chiefly confined to those which are hortatory in character.

Probably few have realized with more fulness the spiritual nature of Christianity than did Isaac Penington. His own relation of what befell him in his pursuit after truth cannot fail, therefore, to be deeply instructive.

"I was acquainted," he says, "with a spring of life from my childhood, which enlightened me in my tender years, and pointed my heart towards the Lord, begetting true sense in me, and faith, and hope, and love, and humility, and meekness, &c., so that indeed I was a wonder to some that knew me, because of the savor and life of religion which dwelt in my heart and appeared in my conversation.

"But I never durst trust the spring of my life, and the springings up of life therefrom; but, in reading the Scriptures, gathered what knowledge I could therefrom, and set this over the spring and springings of life in me, and indeed judged that I ought so to do.

"Notwithstanding which, the Lord was very tender and merciful to me, helping me to pray, and helping me to understand the Scriptures, and opening and warming my heart every day.

"And truly my soul was very near the Lord, and my heart was made and preserved very low and humble before him, and very sensible of his rich love and mercy to me in the Lord Jesus Christ; as I did daily from my heart cry grace. grace, unto him, in every thing my soul received and partook of from him.

"Indeed, I did not look to have been so broken, shattered. and distressed as I afterwards was, and could by no means understand the meaning thereof, my heart truly and earnestly desiring after the Lord, and not having the sense of any guilt upon me. Divers came to see me, some to inquire into and consider of my condition: others to bewail it. and if possible administer some relief, help, and comfort to me: and divers were the judgments they had concerning me. Some would say it was deep melancholy; others would narrowly search. and inquire how, and in what manner. and in what way, I had walked. and were jealous that I had sinned against the Lord and provoked him some way or other, and that some iniquity lay as a load upon me; but, after thorough converse with me, they would still express that they were of another mind, and that the hand of the Lord was in it, and it was an eminent case, and would end in good to my soul.

"At that time, when I was broken and dashed to pieces in my religion, I was in a congregational way, but soon after parted with them, yet in great love, relating to them how the hand of the Lord was upon me, and how I was smitten in the inward part of my religion, and could not now hold up an outward form of that which I inwardly wanted, having lost my God, my Christ, my faith, my knowledge. my life, my all. And so we parted very lovingly, I wishing them well, even the presence of that God whom I wanted. promising to return to them again if ever I met with that which my soul wanted, and had clearness in the Lord so to do.

"After I was parted from them, I never joined to any way or people; but lay mourning day and night, pleading with the Lord why he had forsaken me, and why I should be made so miserable through my love to him and sincere desires after him. For truly I can say. I had not been capable of so much misery as my soul lay in for many years, had not my love been so deep and true towards the Lord my God. and my desires so great after the sensible enjoyment of his spirit according to the promise and way of the gospel. Yet this I can also say, in uprightness of heart: it was not gifts I desired. to appear and shine before men in; but grace and holiness. and the spirit of the Lord dwelling in me, to act my heart by his grace. and to preserve me in holiness.

"Now indeed the Lord at length had compassion on me, and visited me, though in a time and way wherein I expected him not; nor was I willing, as to the natural part. to have that the way which God showed me to be the way; but the Lord opened my eye, and that which I knew to be of him in me closed with it and owned it; and the pure seed was raised by his power, and my heart taught to know and own the seed, and to bow and worship before the Lord in the pure power which was then in my heart. So that of a truth I sensibly knew and felt my Saviour, and was taught by him to take up the cross, and to deny that understanding, knowledge, and wisdom which had so long stood in my way; and then I learned that lesson, being really taught it of the Lord, what it is to become a fool for Christ's sake. I cannot say but I had learned somewhat of it formerly; but I never knew how to keep to what I had learned till that day.

"And then God showed me by degrees, as He nurtured me up in the heavenly sense and experience of His spirit, the workings of the good in me, and the workings of the subtlety; and how Himself had, in times past, taught me to pray, and to understand the Scriptures, and to believe in His Son, and to know some things aright; but, withal, how a knowledge and understanding of another nature had crept in and gained ground upon me,—which indeed I knew not how to distinguish thoroughly from the other and watch against; and so the Truth came not to live in me, nor I to live in that, according to the utmost desire and travail of my soul.

"But now of a truth, by this blessed visitation of the everlasting gospel, the Lord hath at length brought me back to the same spring I was acquainted with at first, and joined my heart in true sense and understanding to it; so that the life that I live is by the springing up of life in me: and I know the Lord my God, by being daily taught by Him so to do; and I love Him, by feeling my heart circumcised and constrained through the new nature thereunto. And truly it is natural to the good seed in me, and to my soul in and through the same, to trust my Father, and to suffer any thing that He requires of me, who freely giveth me both to do and to suffer; for indeed I live not of myself, but by a continual gift, and quickening of life in my heart.

"And oh that others could also come to hear the testimony of truth and life from God's Holy Spirit, and be turned thereby to the pure principle and spirit of life itself, (which many formerly had a true taste of, but are now turned aside to another nature and spirit, though they themselves know it not,) that they might witness the gospel-power, and know the spiritual and heavenly Jerusalem who is the mother and bringer-up of all that are truly living!"

At another time he writes, "But some may desire to know what I have at last met with; I answer, *I have met with the Seed*. Understand that word, and thou wilt be satisfied, and inquire no further. I have met with my God. I have met with my Saviour; and he hath not been present with me without his salvation, but I have felt the healings drop upon my soul from under his wings; I have met with the true knowledge, the knowledge of life, the living knowledge, the knowledge which is life, and this hath had the true virtue in it, which my soul hath rejoiced in, in the presence of the Lord. I have met with the true spirit of prayer and supplication, wherein the Lord is prevailed with, and which draws from him whatever the condition needs, the soul always looking up to him in the will, and in the time and way which is acceptable with him. What shall I say? I have met with the true peace, the true righteousness, the true holiness, the true rest of the soul, the everlasting habitation, which the redeemed dwell in. And I know all these to be true, in Him that is true, and am capable of no doubt, dispute, or reasoning in my mind about them, it abiding there where it hath received the full assurance and satisfaction. And also I know very well and distinctly in spirit, where the doubts and disputes are, and where the certainty and full assurance is, and in the tender mercy of the Lord am preserved out of the one, and in the other."

So devoted was Isaac Penington to the service of his Master, that, in common with many of his fellow-members, he was forced to undergo the punishment of human law for fulfilling what he believed to be the commands of the divine. Six times he was taken to jail for declining to take oaths, or for meeting with his friends to worship in a mode not approved by the Established Church, and in these imprisonments spent nearly five years of his life. It also appears that certain designing relatives, knowing their conscientious scruple against swearing, had involved him and his wife in a suit in chancery, where their answer without an oath was invalid. This resulted in the loss of his estate; and during one of the terms of his imprisonment his family were turned out of his house by the parties who had seized it, and were forced thenceforward to depend upon the property of his wife for their subsistence. But through these manifold trials his faith was firm. Having surrendered his will to his Maker, and having entered the path of duty, in quest of that happiness which he knew existed not elsewhere, he was enabled, while running the race, to keep in sight the crown which lay at the end.

While we feel that an adequate impression of Isaac Penington's character cannot be conveyed within the limits of a short preface, yet we can but refer to one feature of it which held a marked prominence. We allude to the strong current of his sympathies towards any who might be suffering mental or spiritual distress. Having himself lived through weary years of loneliness of spirit, his heart was ready to be touched by the condition of those who in darkness were longing for the light of truth. So deep was at times the tenderness of his sorrowing solicitude on behalf of these, that his whole soul seemed to enter into feeling with them; and among the letters here published there are several which bear witness to the zeal of his endeavors to point them to the way of life.

The following extract from a testimony concerning him, written by his friend Thomas Ellwood, beautifully portrays his Christian character:—

"As he had freely received of the Lord, so did he freely and readily communicate thereof, as the following sheets do witness, unto such as stood in need of counsel, advice, information, or direction in their travel to the heavenly country. To which service he was fitted, and very well furnished by the experiences of his own travel; for the Lord had led him through many a strait and difficulty, through many temptations, trials, and exercises, by which He had tried and proved him: not only through the Red Sea and the wilderness had he passed, but the bottom of Jordan also had he seen, and the upholding, delivering arm of the Lord through all he had known and felt; whereby he was able to speak a word of information to the bewildered passenger, a word of encouragement to the weary and fainting traveller, a word of comfort to the afflicted soul, and of consolation to the wounded spirit. And oh, how sweetly have I heard it flow from him! how has it dropped like the dew and distilled like the gentle rain! Ah, how tender, how compassionate, how full of bowels and feeling sympathy was he! Surely His words have been many times like apples of gold in pictures of silver. For of a truth the Lord was with him, and his heavenly power did often fill his Temple; and the spirit of the Lord rested upon him, and the fruits thereof were plentifully brought forth through him in love, in joy, in peace, in long-suffering, in gentleness, in goodness, in faith, in meekness, and in temperance, so richly did the word of the Lord dwell in him. His delight was in the service of God, to which he was wholly given up, and in it spent most of his time, either publicly in meetings waiting upon God, or privately in visiting and ministering unto those that were distressed or anyway afflicted in mind or body; and, when at home, he was frequent in retirements and very inward with the Lord. Very fervent he was in prayer, and very frequent; for the spirit of grace and supplication was plentifully poured upon him, by which he often wrestled with the Lord, and not in vain. The Holy Scriptures he read much, and with great delight and profit; for he made it not a cursory or formal business, nor sought to pick out the meaning by his natural wit or learning, but, with a great composedness of mind and reverence of spirit, waited to receive the true sense of them from the openings of that Divine Spirit by which the penmen of them were inspired. Great and strong was the travail of his spirit for the conversion of others, and in a more especial manner did his love flow and bowels yearn after the professors of religion, for whom he continually and earnestly labored both by word and writing, not ceasing to seek them to his dying day, that they might be brought off from the shadows and come at length to inherit substance. And, blessed be the Lord, by the powerful operation of the Spirit of God, through his ministry many were turned to the truth and many confirmed in it; for the Lord was with him, and spake by him, so that his teaching was with divine authority, in the demonstration of the spirit and of power. To the world and the affairs of it he was very much a stranger, but deeply experienced in the things of God: for, his affection being set on things above, his conversation was in heaven, and his life hid with Christ in God He was but a pilgrim on the earth, and is now gone home."

# CONTENTS.

| LETTER | | PAGE |
|---|---|---|
| I. | Of a Growth in Grace amidst Distressing Exercises of Spirit. *To Bridget Atley*............... | 13 |
| II. | The Compassion of the Shepherd of the Flock towards the Weak, &c.—How they should follow Him. *To Friends*.................................. | 16 |
| III. | On Searching after the Hidden Treasure and Selling all for it. *To Catherine Pordage*....... | 18 |
| IV. | The Duty of being Content with what is made known................................................ | 21 |
| V. | On Faith in the Healing Power of Christ......... | 23 |
| VI. | Advice to One respecting the Dark Suggestions of the Enemy...................................... | 25 |
| VII. | On True Judgment, and on Prejudices; also on the Variety of Gifts and Stations in the Church. *To Friends of Truth in and about the Two Chalfonts*................................. | 28 |
| VIII. | The Day of God's Power and Love. *To John Mannock*........................................... | 31 |
| IX. | On Simplicity of Faith and Dedication. *To John Mannock*...................................... | 37 |
| X. | Advice and Sympathy under Trial. *To Elizabeth Walmsley*...................................... | 40 |

## CONTENTS.

| LETTER | | PAGE |
|---|---|---|
| XI. | Of Obedience in Confessing Christ; also on the Light of Christ. *To Elizabeth Stonar*.................................................. | 41 |
| XII. | Encouragement to Faithfulness under Apprehension of Sufferings. *To Widow Hemmings.*............................................ | 43 |
| XIII. | Exhortation relative to the Christian Life and Travel. *To Dulcibella Layton*....... | 45 |
| XIV. | Comfort and Counsel to One under Affliction. *To the Lady Conway*.............. | 47 |
| XV. | On the Benefit of Chastening by Afflictions. *To the Lady Conway*........................ | 49 |
| XVI. | On being ingrafted into Christ, being preserved alive in Him, and growing up to Him in all things. *To S. W.*............... | 53 |
| XVII. | Counsel to One tossed as with Tempests.... | 58 |
| XVIII. | Encouragement under Trials incident to Bearing the Cross of Christ................... | 60 |
| XIX. | On being offended with those who fall into Temptation................................................ | 61 |
| XX. | On Shunning the Cross. *To Catherine Pordage*........................................... | 63 |
| XXI. | On Love, Meekness, and Watching over each other. *To Friends in Amersham*... | 64 |
| XXII. | On the Spiritual Appearance of Christ...... | 66 |
| XXIII. | To One under Divine Visitation................ | 67 |
| XXIV. | Encouragement to look up to the Lord amidst His Chastenings, and the Smitings of the Enemy......................................... | 69 |
| XXV. | On Unreserved Obedience. *To Bridget Atley*............................................. | 72 |
| XXVI. | Afflictions may Work out a Weight of | |

| LETTER | | PAGE |
|---|---|---|
| | Glory. *To my Dear Suffering Friends in Scotland* | 75 |
| XXVII. | An Invitation to Heavenly Substance. | 78 |
| XXVIII. | Advice respecting Church Discipline. *To the Women's Meeting of Friends in the Truth at John Mannock's* | 80 |
| XXIX. | Of Preservation and a Growth in the Heavenly Life—Its Power over the Earthly Nature. *To the single, upright-hearted, and faithful Friends of Truth in and about the two Chalfonts* | 84 |
| XXX. | On the True, Living, Heavenly Knowledge. *To the Lady Conway* | 91 |
| XXXI. | On Disputation, and on Hearing Wisdom's Voice; also respecting the Puritan State. *To E. Terry* | 94 |
| XXXII. | Advice as to Self-deceit on the Unity of the Spirit—The Younger are to submit to the Elder. *To Miles Stanclif* | 97 |
| XXXIII. | The Loving-Kindness of the Lord. *To Elizabeth Walmsley, of Giles-Chalfont* | 99 |
| XXXIV. | On the Danger of Self-Complacency. *To Catherine Pordage.* | 100 |
| XXXV. | Acknowledgment of Christ's Manhood. *To Richard Roberts* | 102 |
| XXXVI. | The Way to Life Narrow—Hard Things made Easy to the Obedient—Also some Answers to Objections on Prayer, &c. *To Catherine Pordage* | 105 |
| XXXVII. | The Scriptures exceedingly Precious—The Gospel a Ministration of the Spirit of | |

| LETTER | | PAGE |
|---|---|---|
| | Life in Christ Jesus—The Liability of Losing the Sense and Savor of this....... | 111 |
| XXXVIII. | The Unsearchable Riches of Christ.—Believers may Partake thereof through Obedience, and be Preserved from every Harm. *To Friends of both the Chalfonts.* | 116 |
| XXXIX. | Faithful Dealing between Brethren recommended................................. | 124 |

# LETTERS OF ISAAC PENINGTON.

## LETTER I.

OF A GROWTH IN GRACE AMIDST DISTRESSING EXERCISES OF SPIRIT.

*To Bridget Atley.*

MY DEAR FRIEND:—

If thy heart come to feel the seed of God, and to wait upon him in the measure of his life, he will be tender of thee as a father of his child, and his love will be naturally breaking forth towards thee. This is the end of all his dealings with thee, to bring thee hither, to make thee fit and capable of entering and abiding here. And he hath changed, and doth change thy spirit daily; though it be as the shooting up of the corn, whose growth cannot be discerned at present by the most observing eye, but it is very manifest afterwards that it hath grown. My heart is refreshed for thy sake, rejoicing in the Lord's goodness towards thee; and that the blackness of darkness begins to scatter from thee, though the enemy be still striving the same way to enter and distress thee again. But wait to feel the relieving measure of life, and heed not distressing thoughts, when they arise ever so strongly in thee; nay, though they have entered thee, fear them not, but *be still a while, not believing in the power which thou feelest they have over thee*, and it will fall on a sudden.

It is good for thy spirit, and greatly to thy advantage, to be much and variously exercised by the Lord. Thou dost not know what the Lord hath already done, and what he is yet doing for thee therein. Ah! how precious it is to be poor, weak, low, empty, naked, distressed for Christ's sake, that way may be made for the power and glory of his life in the heart! And, oh, learn, daily more and more, to trust him and hope in him, and not to be affrighted with any amazement, nor to be taken up with the sight of the present thing; but wait for the shutting of thy own eye upon every occasion, and for the opening of the eye of God in thee, and for the sight of things therewith, as they are from him. It is no matter what the enemy strives to do in thy heart, nor how distressed thy condition is, but what the Lord will do for thee, which is with patience to be waited for at his season in every condition. And though sin overtake, let not that bow down; nor let the eye open in thee, which stands poring at that: but wait for the healing through the chastisement, and know there is an Advocate, who, in that hour, hath an office of love and a faithful heart towards thee. Yea, though thou canst not believe, yet be not dismayed thereat; thy Advocate, who undertakes thy cause, hath faith to give: only do thou sink into, or at least pant after the hidden measure of life, which is not in that which distresseth, disturbeth, and filleth thee with thoughts, fears, troubles, anguish, darknesses, terrors, and the like; no, no! but in that which inclines to the patience, to the stillness, to the hope, to the waiting, to the silence before the Father: this is the same in nature, with the most refreshing and glorious-visiting life, though not the same in appearance; and, if thy mind be turned to it, not minding but overlooking the other, thou wilt find some of the same virtue springing up in thy heart and soul, at least to stay thee.

In and through these things, thou wilt become deeply acquainted with the nature of God, and know the wonderful riches and virtue of his life, the mightiness of his power, and the preciousness of his love, tenderness of his mercy, and infiniteness of his wisdom, the glory also, and exactness of his righteousness, &c.: thou wilt be made large in spirit to receive and drink in abundantly of them; and the snares of the enemy will be so known to thee and discerned, the way of help so manifest and easy, that their strength will be broken, and the poor entangled bird will fly away singing, from the nets and entanglements of the fowler; and praises will spring up, and great love in thy heart to the Forgiver and Redeemer. Oh, wait, hope, trust, look up to thy God! look over that which stands between; come into his mercy! let in the faith which openeth the way of life, which will shut out the distrusting and doubting mind, and will close up the wrong eye, that letteth in reasonings and temptations, the wrong sense, and death with them.

Thus mayest thou witness, in and through thy Redeemer, the abundance of his life and peace.

I. P.

## LETTER II.

### THE COMPASSION OF THE SHEPHERD OF THE FLOCK TOWARDS THE WEAK, ETC.—HOW THEY SHOULD FOLLOW HIM.

*To Friends.*

He that is weak and foolish among the lambs, continually ready to wander, both out of the pastures and from the fold, and thus to betray his life into the hands of the enemy;—he who is continually scattering and squandering away what the Lord in mercy gathers for him, and freely bestows upon him; who, through drowsiness and carelessness, hath lost the benefit of, and forfeited the sweet and tender visitations of the Most High, and is now become dry, dead, barren, thick, earthy;—O my God! let *that* soul feel the stirrings of the springs of life, and find some encouragements from thee, to hope in the free and large mercies of the Shepherd of Israel; who casteth not off his sheep because of their wanderings, because of their backslidings, because of their infirmities, because of their diseases, nay, not because of their hardness; but pursues them with his love, findeth them out, visiteth with his correcting hand according to their need, woundeth with his sword, and melteth in his fire, until he hath made them tender and pliable, and then he pours in the fresh oil of his salvation and sweetly healeth them.

O my friends and brethren in the pure life! be faithful to the Lord in returning him all the incomes of his Spirit; follow on in every drawing of his love, while any of the virtue of it lasts upon your spirits. Walk with him all the day long, and wait for him all the night season. And, in case of erring from him, or sinning grievously against him, be not discouraged; for he is a God of mercies, and delighteth in pardoning and forgiving much and very often. What tender mother can be more ready to forgive and embrace the child, that appears broken and afflicted with her sore displeasure! Yea, He gives brokenness, He melteth the heart, that he may be tender towards, and embrace it in his arms of reconciliation, and in the peace of his Spirit.

O my dear companions, and fellow-travellers in spirit towards the land of the living! *all* the motions of the life are cross to the corrupt [part]—dwell [in the life,] draw the yoke close about your necks, that ye may come into unity with the life, and the corrupt be worn out. Take the yoke, the cross, the contrariety of Jesus upon your spirits daily; that that may be worn out which hinders the unity, and so, ye may feel your King and Saviour exalted upon his throne in your hearts: this is your rest, peace, life, kingdom, and crown forever.         I. P.

---

## LETTER III.

#### ON SEARCHING FOR THE HIDDEN TREASURE, AND SELLING ALL FOR IT.

*To Catherine* Pordage.

FRIEND :—

Thy estate and condition hath been pretty much with me since I last saw thee. I am sensible how hard it is for thee, to give up to be reached by the seed and power of life; how readily and easily thy ear and heart is opened to another, and the adulterer entertained, who hunteth after the precious life. This word of advice hath been much in my heart to thee this morning: sit down and count the cost of ploughing up thy field, and of searching after the hidden treasure of pure and true wisdom, and consider seriously, whether thou canst sell all for it, both inward and outward riches; that, if thou do set thy hand to the plough, thou mayest not look back after any thing else, within or without, but mayest be content and satisfied with the pearl of true wisdom and life alone.

Now, if thou be truly willing in God's sight thus

to do, thou must singly give up to follow the Lord in the leadings of his Spirit, out of all the ways of thy own wisdom and knowledge, out of all things wherein thou hast a life and delight out of him; thou must not determine what thou hast a life in, but the Lord must search thy heart, and he will soon show thee (if thy heart be naked and open before him, willing to hear and learn of him) somewhat in thy heart, somewhat in thy ways, somewhat in thy words, thoughts, &c. which is contrary to his pure life and Spirit; and then, that must be denied and given up immediately. And afterwards, perhaps the Lord will soon discover to thee another lover, which hath had more of thy heart than thou hast been aware of; and so, thou must part with one after another, until thou hast parted with all: and this will prepare thee for the bosom of thy Beloved, who is a jealous God, and seeth not with the eye wherewith man seeth. But, if thou be not thus singly given up, though thou should put thy hand to the plough, thou wilt be looking back some time or other: and that wisdom which draweth aside from the Lord will blind thy eye and deceive thy mind, and draw thee from the simplicity and nakedness of Truth, into some image or other of it, so that, instead of the pure Truth itself, thou wilt believe and embrace a lie.

Thou hast travelled long in the heights above the seed; Oh, consider, if that be not yet standing in thee, which could not have been found standing, if thou hadst known the true seed, and travelled therewith. This enhances the price of Truth as to thee, that thou must part with more for it, than will be required of many others; yet, if thou be faithful to the Lord, and diligently follow him in the simplicity, Truth will at length recompense thee for all thy labors, sorrows, and travels. But a thorough work will the Lord make in thy earth, if thou singly give up unto him, and faithfully follow; and many devices wilt thou meet with, to turn thy mind out of the way, and to cause thee to shun the bitterness of the cross, and to kindle and nourish a hope in thee, that thou mayest find a more easy way to the same life and everlasting substance. The Lord hath reached to thee, and the Lord is willing to search thy heart, to find out the deceiver and enemy in his most secret lurking-places; but, when the Lord hath found him out, thou must give him up to God's stroke, and not suffer him to find a shelter in thy mind to save him therefrom. For he is very subtle, and will twist and twine all manner of ways to deceive thee and save himself; nor art thou yet acquainted with, or able to discern his devices. The Lord alone can help thee; and he will help thee, if thou be not hasty to join with the enemy, nor give up thy judgment to believe what he represents, and seems inwardly to represent to thee as true; but abide and dwell in the sense of thy own inability to judge, waiting to feel that which is true, pure, and living of God, judge in thee, not so much in demonstrations of wisdom, as tender and secret drawings of the beginnings of a new nature, away from what is of an earthly nature. For thou must come out of the spirit of this world, if thou wilt come into God's Spirit; and thou must come out of the love of the things of this world, if thou wilt come out of the spirit of this world; for, in the love of the things of this world, the spirit of this world lodgeth and dwelleth, and thou canst not touch the unclean thing, but thou also touchest somewhat of the unclean spirit. Therefore, said John, from a true and deep understanding, "Love not the world, neither the things of the world," (if thou love the things of the world, thou lovest the world,) for, "if any man love the world, the love of the Father is not in him."

The day of God's mercy and visitation is upon thee, who is visiting that spirit in thee which hath led thee aside, even with the judgment proper for it; that Zion in thee might be thereby redeemed, and thy soul converted to, and truly brought forth in righteousness.    I. P.

11th of First Month, 1670.

## LETTER IV.

#### THE DUTY OF BEING CONTENT WITH WHAT IS MADE KNOWN.

THE enemy kindles a great distress in the mind, by stirring up an earnest desire, and a sense of a seeming necessity, to *know*. When a motion ariseth, how shall I do, to know whether it be of God or no? For, if it be of God, it ought to be obeyed; and, if it be not of God, it ought to be resisted; but what shall I do, who cannot tell what it is? I must of necessity fall, either into disobedience to God's Spirit, or into the snares of the enemy. Thus the enemy raiseth up a strength in the reasoning part, even unanswerable there. But what if it be better for thee, at present, to be darkened about these things, than as yet to know? Can that possibly be? will the strong reason readily say. Yes, that it may, in many respects. There is somewhat else would live and be acting in thee, if the clear and heavenly knowledge were given; and thou wouldst be centring in self that which thou receivedst from God; yea, thou wouldst miss of the way of true knowledge, and never learn in every state to be content, nor know the pure way and actings of life in such a state. Truly, this is not the way of the child's knowing; but the child knows, in resignation and subjection of its very knowledge; and if there appear ever so great a necessity of knowledge, and yet knowledge be not given, it sinks, in fear and humility, into the will of the pure seed; and there somewhat springs up (unknown to the natural wisdom, and not in the way of man's wisdom) which at seasons preserves and bears it up in such a state. But this is a great mystery; yet sensibly experienced by the true travellers at this day.

Therefore, retire out of all necessities, according to the apprehension of the reasoning mind; and judge that only necessary, which God, in his eternal wisdom and love, proportions out unto us. And when thou comest hither, thou wilt come to thy rest; and as thou abidest here, thou wilt abide in thy soul's true rest, and know the preciousness of that lesson, and of whom thou art to learn it, even, *in every state to be content.* I. P.

---

## LETTER V.

#### ON FAITH IN THE HEALING POWER OF CHRIST.

Friend :—

I have had of late some deep and serious thoughts concerning thee, and a sense of thee, as between the Lord and my own soul, yet I have not had any thing to signify or express to thee, till this morning. But somewhat this morning sprang up in my heart, sweetly and freshly, which I had pure drawings to impart to thee.

There was a quick sense of thee upon my heart, and in that sense this cry was in me :—Oh that thou wert acquainted with the pure, eternal power of the Lord, and mightst feel his outstretched arm revealed in thee, and witness the faith which stands in that power; and, in that faith, believe and wait for what God is doing, and willing to do, in and for his children. "If ye had faith," said Christ, "but as a grain of mustard-seed, ye should say to this mountain, Be thou cast into the midst of the sea, and it should be so." Indeed, the true faith, the pure faith, the living faith, which stands in the power, doth remove all the mountains that are in the way, and makes the crooked ways straight, and the rough ways plain. If thou had lived in the days of Christ's flesh, and wanted outward healing, and had been willing to come to him for healing, but withal had not come with faith that he was able and willing to heal perfectly, mightest not thou have missed of that cleansing and outward health and salvation, which others met with? For, did not he say, "Be it unto thee according to thy faith"? And is not he the Physician of the soul? and is not his skill to be trusted and believed in? He that hopeth, and believeth, and waiteth, and prayeth, and fighteth the good fight of faith, which gives victory over sin, Satan, and the world,—he may possibly overcome; yea, he that warreth lawfully, (that is, with the spiritual weapon, which is mighty through God,) he that warreth with this only, and with this constantly, shall be sure to overcome. For greater is He that is in the true believer, than he that is in the world.

Oh that thou mightest have experience of these things, and witness the banner of Christ's love and power displayed in thee, and the victories and conquests that are thereby, and the safety and peace which is under it! For, of a truth, we do not speak boastingly, but are witnesses of the majesty of God's love and power, which we testify of. The Lord so enlighten and guide thee, that thou mayest obtain the desires of thy heart; for I really believe thy desire is after holiness and after communion with the Father and the Son, and with the saints in light: Oh that thou mayest be led into the true pure light of life, that there thou mayest enjoy what in this kind thou desirest!

This is from one, who singly, as in the Lord's sight, wisheth well unto thee.  I. P.

READING JAIL, 27th of Eighth Month, 1670.

## LETTER VI.

### ADVICE TO ONE RESPECTING THE DARK SUGGESTIONS OF THE ENEMY.

DEAR FRIEND:—

Thou hast had the path of salvation faithfully testified of to thee, and hast come to a sense of the thing; even to the feeling of *that*, whereby the Father begets life, and manifesteth his love and peace, in and to the soul. Now, what remains? but that thou look up to the Lord, to guide thy feet in this path, and to preserve from that which darkens and leads out of the way; that thou mayest pass on thy journey safely, and come to the inheritance and enjoyment of that which thy soul longeth after.

There is life, there is peace, there is joy, there is righteousness, there is health, there is salvation, there is power of redemption, in the seed: yea, there is so. But thy soul wants, and doth not enjoy these things. Well, but how mayest thou come to enjoy them? There is no way, but union with the seed, knowing the seed, hearing the voice of the seed, learning of, and becoming subject to, the seed. "Learn of me, take my yoke upon you," saith Christ, "and ye shall find rest to your souls." Wouldst thou feel thy soul's rest in Christ? Thou must know the seed's voice, hear it, learn daily of him, become his disciple; take up from *his* nature what is contrary to *thy* nature. And then, as thy nature is worn out, and his nature comes up in thee, thou wilt find all easy; all that is of life easy, and transgression hard—unbelief hard: yea, thou wilt find it very hard and unnatural, when the nature of the seed is grown up in thee, either to distrust the Lord or hearken to his enemy. And then thou wilt change that dwelling-place (into which Satan brings dark thoughts, suggestions, and reasonings) for the dwelling-place which is from above, which is the habitation of the righteous; wherein there is light, life, peace, satisfaction, health, salvation, and rejoicing of soul, from and before the Lord.

Now, do not say, Who shall do thus for me? but know, the arm of the Lord is mighty, and brings mighty things to pass; and that arm hath been revealed in thee, and is at work for thee. Oh that thou couldst trust it! (why canst thou not? hath it not sown a seed of faith in thee?) and come into and abide in the path, wherein its mighty, powerful operations are felt and made manifest! And oh that thou mayest find ability to watch against that which bows down, and not so let in, as thou hast done exceedingly, to the grievous wounding and distressing of thy soul! For the enemy's dark suggestions work according to their nature, and if thou let them lie upon thee, how can they but darken, afflict, and perplex thee?

Therefore, in the evil hour, fly from all things that thus arise in thee; and lie still, feel thy stay, till his light, which " makes manifest," arise in thee, and clear up things to thee. And think not the time of darkness long; but watch that thy heart be kept empty, and thy mind clear of thoughts and belief of things till he bring in somewhat, which thou mayest safely receive. Therefore, say to thy thoughts and to thy belief of things, (according to the representation of the dark power, in the time of thy darkness,) "Get thee hence!" And if that will not do, look up to the Lord to speak to them, and to keep them out, if they be not already entered, or to thrust them out, if they be already got in. And, if he do not so presently, or for a long time, yet do not murmur or think much, but wait till he do. Yea, though they violently thrust themselves upon thee, and seem to have entered thy mind, yet let them be as strangers to thee; receive them not, believe them not, know them not, own them not; and thy bosom will, notwithstanding, be chaste in the eye of the Lord, though they may seem to thee to have defiled thee.

Look up to the Father, that thou mayest learn this of him: and, becoming faithful to him therein, thou wilt find thy darkness abate, and its strength more and more broken in thee; and thou wilt not only feel and taste a little now and then, but also come to possess and inherit, and rejoice before the Lord in thy portion.

Thy friend in the Truth which changeth not, but is pure, and preserveth pure forever.   I. P.

From AYLESBURY JAIL, 28th of Seventh Month, 1667.

---

## LETTER VII.

ON TRUE JUDGMENT, AND ON PREJUDICES; ALSO ON THE VARIETY OF GIFTS AND STATIONS IN THE CHURCH.

*To Friends of Truth in and about the two Chalfonts.**

As a father watcheth over his children, so do I wait and desire to feel the Lord watching over my soul continually. And in his love, care, wise and tender counsel, is my safety, life, and peace, and I never yet repented either waiting for him or hearken-

---

* I. P. and his wife appear to have been instrumental in gathering the Friends of that neighborhood to the knowledge of the Truth, as held by the Society.

ing to him. But if I have hearkened at any time to any thing else, and mistook his voice, and entertained the enemy's deceitful appearance, instead of his pure Truth, (which it is very easy to do,) that grievous mistake hath proved matter of loss and sorrow to my soul.

Now, oh my Friends, that ye might know and hear the voice of the Preserver! so shall ye be preserved, and kept from the voice of the stranger, which draweth aside from the pure principle of life, and the true feeling sense. There is that near you which watcheth to betray: Oh, the God of my life, joy, peace, and hope, watch over your souls, and deliver you from the advantages which, at any time, it hath against any of you. The seed which God hath sown in you is pure and precious. Oh that it may be found living in you, and ye abiding in it! Oh that no other seed may, at any time, usurp authority over it! but that ye may know the authority and pure Truth which is of God, and therein stand, in the pure dominion, over all that is against him. For, in the principle of life, which ye have known and received in measure, is dominion; and ye, therein preserved, are in the dominion over the impure and deceitful one; and that judging in you hath power to judge all impurity and deceivableness, as the light thereof pleaseth to make it manifest to you; but, out of that, ye will easily become a prey, and set up darkness for light, and account light darkness; and then, a wrong wisdom, confidence, and conceitedness, will get up in you, and lead you far out of the way and spirit of Truth. O my dear friends, that that may be kept down in you, which is forward to judge, to approve or disapprove; and may the weighty judgment of the seed be waited for! And, oh, do not judge, do not judge, before the light of the day shine in you, and give forth the judgment; but stand and walk in fear and humility, and tenderness of spirit, and silence of flesh, that the Lord be not provoked against any of you, to give you up to a wrong sense and judgment, to the hurt of your souls. And mind your own states, and the feeling of life in your own vessels; which will keep you pure, precious, and chaste in the eye of the Lord. And, oh, do not meddle with talking about others, which eats out the inward life, and may exalt your spirits out of your place, and above your proper growth: be as the weaned child, simple, naked, meek, humble, tender; easily led by and subjected to the Father; so will ye grow in that which is of God, and be preserved out of that which hunteth after the pure life to betray and destroy it. I have an interest in you,—my cries are to the Lord for you, and I exceedingly thirst after your preservation and growth in that which is pure; and in that breathing, longing spirit towards you, was it in my heart at this time to write unto you.

The Lord God of my mercies, hope, and life watch over you for good, and keep your hearts in the pure and single watch, that the enemy, by any subtle device of his, break not in upon you, nor ye, by any temptation, be allured or drawn from the Lord; but may know the pure, eternal, everlasting habitation, and may dwell and abide therein, to the joy of your own souls, and the rejoicing of the hearts of all that have travailed for you in the Spirit of the Lord.

From your brother and companion in the faith, patience, and afflictions of the seed,     I. P.

AYLESBURY PRISON,
25th of Eleventh Month, 1666.

## LETTER VIII.

### THE DAY OF GOD'S POWER AND LOVE.

*To John Mannock.*

FRIEND :—

Hath the Lord drawn thy heart to bear the sound of Truth, and given thee some sense and savor thereof; though, perhaps, not as yet full satisfaction in all things that are truly and faithfully testified concerning it? Oh, prize this love of God to thee! and watch and pray, and come into the pure fear, that thou mayst walk worthy of it, and mayst discern in spirit what it is that gives thee the savor, and so receive the leaven of the kingdom, and feel its leavening virtue upon thy heart day by day. For, after the Lord hath been at work, the enemy will be at work also; and thou mayst both meet with him without, and within too, in reasonings and questionings against the demonstrations of God's Spirit to thy heart and conscience. Now, if thou wilt hearken to these, they will eat out the sense and belief of what God's Spirit begat in thee. Oh, how many wise men, and how many knowing men, that have tasted of some true experiences, have not the sense and discerning of the Spirit and power of the Lord, as it is now made manifest, but speak hard words and think hard thoughts of his Truth and its precious appearances!

Ah! what are we, any of us, on whom the Lord hath shown his mercy, and whose hearts he toucheth and maketh sensible of his drawings; yea, and not only so, but also gives us to partake of the eternal life and virtue, which he hath hid in his Son from the eyes of all living? We sought it up and down, in the deeps and heights; but the deeps said, It is not in me, and the highest mountain and hill that ever we met with could not bring salvation to us. But, at length, we found the fear of the Lord to be the true wisdom, and that which taught us to depart from evil gave us the true understanding. Now, if any among us are not thus taught, but only own the doctrines of Truth published among us, being thereunto overcome by the demonstration of God's Spirit; yet, for all this, they are not felt by us in the life and unity of the Spirit of the Lord with us; and such, the Lord will manifestly prune off, in his own due time, and graft in others in their stead. Yea, such as do indeed give up to Truth, and in measure feel the power of it, and are made by the power of the Lord subject to it—yet, if in any thing they let in the spirit of the world, and act according thereto, so far they are not of the Truth nor owned by it.

Now, dear friend, (for, so far as thy heart is touched by God's Spirit and answereth thereto, thou art dear unto me,) mind thy condition, and wait on the Lord in humility of heart, and in subjection to what he inwardly, by his Spirit, daily makes manifest; that thou mayest come into the obedience of the Truth daily; that thou mayest daily feel the change which is wrought in the heart and conscience by the holy, eternal, ever-living power; that so thou mayest witness, according to the Scriptures, "that which is born of the Spirit is spirit." And then thou wilt feel that this birth of the Spirit cannot fulfil the lusts of the flesh, but will be warring and fighting the good fight of faith, in the power of life, against them; and thus, in faithfulness to the Truth and waiting upon the Lord, thou shalt witness an overcoming in his due time. For, indeed, the true faith overcomes, the true shield beats down the most fiery darts, and, in the power of the Lord, the enemy is so resisted that he fleeth; and the name of the Lord is, indeed, a strong tower to his children, to which his seed know how to retire and feel safety.

Oh, the conquering faith, the overcoming life and power, of the Spirit! We cannot but speak of those things, and cry up the perfect gift and the power of

Him who is not only able to perfect his work in the heart, but delights so to do, and even to tread down Satan under the feet of those that wait in patience for the perfect conquest; for nothing else will fully satisfy. The rest, the peace, the liberty, the life, the virtue of the gospel is not fully known and enjoyed while there remains any sin to sting and trouble. And this I can faithfully witness,—that when the power is revealed, when the blood washeth, the soul is clean and as white as snow, and the enemy hath not power to break in, but life triumphs over him. And why may there not be a continuance of such a state? Yea, I verily believe, many can witness a continuance of such a state, which the Spirit of the Lord doth not call less in them than a perfect state, a sound state, wherein Christ, the heavenly Physician, hath healed them perfectly, and made them witnesses of true soundness of soul and spirit in the sight of God. Oh that all knew and enjoyed it who truly desire and long after it!

But as for thee, this is in my heart to thee. Thou hast found the pearl: the Lord, in mercy to thee, has discovered to thee the true pearl. Now, this remains,—that thou be a wise merchant, selling all to purchase it. Thou must keep back nothing. Christ, the living Truth, the holy power of righteousness, must be dearer to thee than all. If father, mother, livelihood, liberty, friendship, outward advantages, &c., or any thing else, be dearer to thee than him, he will look upon thee as unworthy of him, and cannot but turn from thee, and suffer hardness and darkness to come again upon thee. Therefore, prize the day of thy visitation from the holy God, from the God of mercy and salvation; and be faithful in the little, in the day of small things, if ever thou desire to enjoy and be ruler over much. The Lord may exercise thee in, and require of thee, little things, as he hath done the rest of the flock, whose footsteps thou art to follow to the Shepherd's tents; and the enemy will be endeavoring to stop thee and perplex thee in every little thing that the Lord requires of thee. But be thou simple like a child, not taking care what to answer wise professors, nor what to answer the reasonings of thy own mind; but, seeing thou hast felt the demonstration of Truth from God's Holy Spirit, oh, breathe unto the Lord to preserve thee in the innocency and simplicity thereof, that the Lord may still be with thee, and thereby bring thee through the day of Jacob's trouble, to taste of Jacob's deliverance and salvation out of trouble: for thou must meet with trials as well as others have done, and the enemy's endeavor will be to make thee stumble and start back in the day of trial. But, if thine eye be towards the Lord, he will uphold and strengthen thee, and bring thee through all that stands in thy way; manifesting to thee daily, more and more, the path of holiness in which the ransomed of the Lord walk, and enabling thee also to walk therein.

Therefore, watch the thoughts and reasonings

which rise in thee, and retire from them, waiting to feel the pure seed and to hear its voice in stillness; whose voice is otherwise than after the noises of the questionings and reasonings which the enemy raiseth in the mind to fill it with doubts and troubles; and to weaken the faith and sense which God wrought in the heart when he reached forth his Truth, in the power and demonstration of his Spirit, unto it. This was God's love, this was the day of his power, which loosens the mind from its lovers and the ways of its own choosing, and begets a willingness to be joined to the Lord and his pure Truth.

Oh, take heed of hearkening to the enemy, to the subtle reasoner, the entangler of the soul! take heed of consulting there, where he lays his baits to entangle the mind and undo the work of God's power in the heart; and so, to make unwilling again, after the Lord had made willing. The steps which the soul takes in the power, even the inclining of the mind towards the Lord and his pure Truth, tend to salvation; but, if any let in unbelief of those things concerning which God had wrought faith in them, they draw back to perdition, they hearken to that which tempts from the Lord, and to him whose end is to destroy them.

This is in true love to thee, and from an upright desire that thou mayest feel the Lord's preservation of thy soul in that which is of him, and his separating thee from all that is not of him.

From a friend to all that breathe after the Lord,

and desire to know and partake of the power and life of Truth as it is in Jesus, the alone Redeemer and Saviour of the soul.
I. P.

3d or 4th of Tenth Month, 1668.

---

## LETTER X.

### ON SIMPLICITY OF FAITH AND DEDICATION.

*To John Mannock.*

Friend :—

It is a wonderful thing to witness the power of God reaching to the heart, and demonstrating to the soul, the pure way of life, as in his sight and presence. Surely, he that partakes of this is therein favored by the Lord, and ought diligently to wait for the giving up to the leadings of his Holy Spirit in every thing; that so he may travel through all that is contrary to the Lord into that nature and spirit which is of Him. It is a wonderful thing, also, to witness God's preservation from backsliding, and from being entangled by the subtlety of the enemy, who hath many ways and taking devices to ensnare the simple mind, and draw it from the sense of Truth into some notions and belief of things wherein the soul may be lulled asleep with hopes and persuasions, but hath not the feeling or enjoyment of the true life and power.

Oh, friend, hast thou a sense of the way to the

Father? then be careful that thy spirit daily bow before him, and wait for breathings to him from his pure Spirit, that he would continue his mercy to thee, keeping thee in the true sense, and making thy way more and more clear before thee every day; yea, and bearing thee up in all the exercises and trials which may befall thee in every kind; that, by his secret working in thy spirit, and helping thee with a little help from time to time, thou mayest still be advancing nearer and nearer towards the kingdom, until thou find the Lord God administer an entrance unto thee thereinto, and give thee an inheritance of life, joy, righteousness, and peace therein; which is strength unto the soul against sin and death, and against the sorrow and trouble which ariseth in the mind for want of God's presence and holy power revealed there.

And be not careful after the flesh, but trust the Lord. What though thou art weak and little; though thou meet with those that are wise and knowing, and almost every way able to reason thee down; what though thou hast not wherewith to answer, yet thou knowest and hast the feeling of God's pure Truth in spirit, with a desire to have the life of it brought forth in thee, and so to witness the change and renewings which are by his power. Oh, dear heart! herein thou art accepted of the Lord, and here his tender love and care will be over thee, and his mercy will daily reach to thee; and thou shalt have true satisfaction in thy heart, and hold the Truth there, where all the reasonings of men, and all the devices of the enemy of thy soul, shall not be able to reach; yea, thou shalt so feel the Lord to help his babe against the strength of the mighty, in the seasons of his good pleasure, as shall exceedingly turn to his praise: and so thou shalt experience that whom God preserves, all the gates of hell shall not be able to prevail against. Therefore look not out at men, or at the words and wisdom of men, but keep where thou hast felt the Lord visit thee, that he may visit thee yet again and again every day, and be teaching thee further and further the way to his dwelling-place, and be drawing thee thither, where is righteousness, life, rest, and peace, forever.

This arose in my heart this morning in tender love towards thee. Look up to the Lord, who can make it useful to thee, to warm, quicken, and strengthen thy heart and mind towards the Lord and his pure Truth, wherewith he has visited thee. And if thou feel any thing therein suitable to the state and condition of thy soul, oh, bow before the Lord, that in the true humility thou mayest confess and give the glory to him of what belongs to him.

From thy friend in the Truth, which cleanseth the heart from iniquity, as it is embraced and dwelt in.

I. P.

23d of Tenth Month, 1668

## LETTER X.

### ADVICE AND SYMPATHY UNDER TRIAL.

*To Elizabeth Walmsley.*

MY VERY DEAR FRIEND :—

Many are the trials, afflictions, and temptations which the Lord seeth good to exercise us with, for the purifying and making us white, that he may honor his name in us and through us: but this promise stands sure in the seed, "I will never leave thee, nor forsake thee." And if our God be with us and for us, what can prevail against the work and design of his love and power towards us?

I am deeply sensible of thy condition, feeling it even in the tender and melting love of my heart towards thee; and this word sprang in me to thee: Look not out, but trust in the Lord, who can make things easier than they seem likely to be, and will certainly carry *his* through the hardest things which he suffers to befall them.

Oh, the Lord keep all in his pure innocency, out of the earthly, contriving wisdom which saith, Save thyself,—avoid this dreadful brunt, this stroke of the cross; which it is easy to hearken to, if the mind be not kept to that eye and that wisdom which discovers the tempter, and instructeth the bird to escape his snare.

My dear love is to thee and to all faithful friends. The Lord keep you from hearkening to the enemy, and make you faithful to him in the pure innocency and heavenly wisdom which is of him; for Truth triumphs over deceit, and the life of the Lamb on the cross reigns and triumphs over death: glory to Him who hath overcome in his person, and who teacheth us to overcome through faith in his power, and from the overflowings of the conquering life in our hearts which first brings down that which is contrary to Truth, and then reigns in the Truth.

Thy friend, in the love which never dies, and in the Truth which changes not. I. P.

CATSGROVE, 14th of Tenth Month, 1670.

---

## LETTER XI.

OF OBEDIENCE IN CONFESSING CHRIST; ALSO ON THE LIGHT OF CHRIST.

*To Elizabeth Stonar.*

DEAR FRIEND :—

I am sensible that the Lord hath visited thee with his power, reaching to thy heart in the demonstration of his own Spirit, and that thy heart hath answered, and said in the inward of thy soul, It is God's Truth, indeed. Now, so far as God hath reached to thee, so far it behooves thee to confess him, his Truth, and people, before men, and to give up in obedience and subjection of spirit to the Lord. And if thou say in the simplicity of thy heart to any that have any tenderness, Thus it is with me: I believe from my heart this or this is of God,—what shall I do? shall I give up in obedience thereto, or shall I disobey the Lord, grieve his Spirit, and wound my own soul? This will reach that which is of God in any, and this will wound and trouble that which is not of God.

The Lord guide thee and pity thee, and help thee in thy straits, and doubts, and fears, and troubles, both in reference to thyself and mother. God is my witness, whom I serve in my spirit in the gospel of his Son, that I have not sought myself, but your good; and that, not of myself neither, but in the leadings and drawings of his Holy Spirit. And I gave thy husband a warning, in true and tender love; though I knew well enough how hard it would be to his spirit in his present state, and what a bitter enemy he might become to me for telling him the truth. I did it not unadvisedly, but in the weight of my spirit before the Lord; and I heartily wish that he were not deceived in heart concerning his own state, but truly knew it, as it is.

Thy soul's true and sincere-hearted friend,

I. P.

## LETTER XII.

#### ENCOURAGEMENT TO FAITHFULNESS UNDER APPREHENSION OF SUFFERINGS.

*To Widow Hemmings.*

My dear Friend :—

I have not forgotten thee, but have often inquired after thee, and many times breathed for thee.

Oh, my friend, look not out at what stands in the way; what if it look dreadfully as a lion, is not the Lord stronger than the mountains of prey? but look *in*, where the law of life is written, and the will of the Lord revealed, that thou mayst know what is the Lord's will concerning thee; and then, show thyself a faithful daughter of Abraham, and be like Sarah, not terrified with any amazement. So soon as I had read thy letter, this arose in my heart to thee, as God's counsel, proper to thy state. Have no fellowship with the unfruitful works of darkness, but rather reprove them. Be not straitened in thy spirit, as fearing what thou shalt suffer for Christ's sake; or, as if God would not stand by thee, or carry thee through. Be thy sufferings as great as possible, yet He is faithful, who hath promised thee an hundredfold in this life.

Oh, what can hurt thee, if thy God stand by thee? Be faithful to his testimony in thy place, and he will stand by thee. Take heed of joining with dead worships, which the seed of God in thee disowns, and cannot relish; but, meekly and in fear, testify against, and abstain from, what thou feelest not to be of the Lord.

This was what was in my heart to thee at present, in true and tender love, and in melting desires for thee, that the Lord may guide and preserve thee, and give thee of the Lamb's courage and strength, who by meekness and sufferings is now to conquer. What if the wicked nature, which is as a sea casting out mire and dirt, rage against thee? There is a river, a sweet, still, flowing river, the streams whereof will make glad thy heart. And learn but in quietness and stillness to retire to the Lord, and wait upon him; in whom thou shalt feel peace and joy, in the midst of thy trouble from the cruel and vexatious spirit of this world. So, wait to know thy work and service to the Lord every day, in thy place and station; and the Lord make thee faithful therein, and thou wilt want neither help, support, nor comfort.

Thy friend, in the truest, sincerest, and most constant love, I. P.

LONDON, 1st of Ninth Month, 1675.

## LETTER XIII.

### EXHORTATION RELATIVE TO THE CHRISTIAN LIFE AND TRAVEL.

*To Dulcibella Laiton.*

Dear Friend :—

Concerning whom I feel a travail,—this is the sense of my heart in relation to thee.

There is a pure seed of life, which God hath sown in thee: oh that it might come through, and come over all that is above it, and contrary to it! And for that end wait daily to feel it, and to feel thy mind subdued by it, and joined to it. Take heed of looking out, in the reasonings of thy mind, but dwell in the feeling sense of life; and then, that will arise in thee more and more, which maketh truly wise, and gives power, and brings into the holy authority and dominion of life. Many that have been long travelling, are now entering into their possessions and inheritance, which the Lord is daily enlarging in them, and to them. Oh that thy lot may be among them, inwardly witnessed and possessed by thee! Prize inward exercises, griefs, and troubles; and let faith and patience have their perfect work in them. Oh, desire to be good, upright, and perfect in God's sight, and wait to feel the life, Spirit, and power, which makes so. Come out of the knowledge and comprehension about things, into the feeling life; and let that be thy knowledge and wisdom, which thou receivest and retainest in the feeling life; and that will lead thee into the footsteps of the flock, without reasoning, consulting, or disputing.

Oh, wait to be taught and enabled by God to fetch right steps in thy travels; and to take up the cross and despise the shame in every thing, wherein that wisdom, will, and mind, which is to be crucified, would be judge; for it will judge amiss, and lead aside, if it be hearkened to by thee. The Lord show thee the snares and dangers to which thou art liable, and lead thee out of them; that whatever hindereth may be discovered to thee, and thy mind singly joined to that which discovereth, that so it may be removed out of the way; and all crooked things be made straight in thee, and the rough plain, and the high low, and the low high, and the weak and foolish strong and wise, and the wise and strong weak and foolish. Oh, wait to feel and understand my words, that thy conversation may be ordered aright by the power and wisdom of God; and that thou mayst inwardly come to witness the glorious coming of Him, who is the salvation of God, and in whom thou shalt not fail to see the salvation of God.

Thou must be very low, weak, and foolish, that the seed may arise in thee to exalt thee, and become thy strength and wisdom; and thou must die exceedingly, again and again, more and more, inwardly and deeply! that thy life may spring up from the holy root and stock; and thou mayst be more and more gathered into it, spring up into it, and live alone in the life, virtue, and power thereof. The travel is long, the exercises many, the snares, temptations, and dangers many; and yet the mercy, relief, and help is great also.

Oh that thou mayst feel thy calling and election, thy sinking down, springing up, and establishment, in the pure seed, in the light and righteousness thereof over all; that thou mayst sing songs of degrees to the Redeemer of Israel, and mayest daily more and more partake of and rejoice in Him, who is our joy, and the crown thereof.

Thy friend, in the most sincere, tender love,

I. P.

11th of Fifth Month, 1677.

## LETTER XIV.

#### COMFORT AND COUNSEL UNDER AFFLICTION.

*To the Lady Conway.*

DEAR FRIEND:—

In tender love, and in a sense of thy sore afflictions and exercises, I do most dearly salute thee; desiring for thee, that the work of the Lord in thy heart may not be interrupted by any devices of the enemy; but that it may go on and prosper in thee, in the springing up of the pure seed of life in thy heart, and in the powerful overturning, by the mighty arm of the Lord, of all that is contrary thereto in thee. Oh that thou mayst daily feel that holy birth of life, which is begotten by the Father, and lives by faith in him!—I say, oh that thou mayst daily feel it living in thee, when temptations and trials on every hand increase—feel the birth of life, which will cry to the Father, "Lord, increase my faith!"

Though sorrows, heaviness, and faintings of heart ever so much increase; yet, if thy faith increase also, it will bear thee up in the midst of them. I would fain have it go well with thee, and that thou mightst not want the Reprover, in any thing that is to be reproved in thee; nor the Comforter, in any respect wherein thy soul wants comfort; nor the holy Counsellor and Adviser, in any strait or difficulty which the wise and tender God orders to befall thee.

Ah that thou mightst come to feel the daily wasting of sin and death, and the daily springing of life and holiness in thy heart! The pearl is worth thousands of worlds, with the greatest earthly glory and pleasure imaginable. Oh that thou mayst be taught of God to discern it more and more, and to buy it, and to come into the enjoyment and possession of it! The Lord manifest Zion more and more to thee, and show thee the glory of it, and set thy feet towards it; and put into thy heart to seek of him the way to it, renewing thee more and more in the spirit of thy mind, whereby the way comes clearly to be discerned, and faithfully walked in; that thou mayst witness, daily, the everlasting covenant of life and peace, even the sure mercies of David.

The desire of my soul is, that thy affections, which how grievous soever, yet are but momentary, may fit thee for, and work out, an eternal weight of glory, for thy soul to inherit in another world, forever.

I remain a sympathizer with thee in thy sufferings; who desires all the advantage and blessings from the God of my life may come to thee, which hardships, temptations, and trials, prepare the heart and make way for.                         I. P.

14th of Twelfth Month, 1678.

---

## LETTER XV.

### ON THE BENEFIT OF CHASTENING BY AFFLICTIONS.

*To the Lady Conway.*

DEAR FRIEND:—

As I was lately retired in spirit and waiting upon the Lord, having a sense on me of thy long, sore, and deep affliction and distress, there arose a Scripture in my heart to lay before thee, namely, Heb. xii. 5, 6, 7, which, I entreat thee, to call for a Bible, and hear read, before thou proceedest to what follows.

Oh, my friend! after it hath pleased the Lord in tender mercy to visit us, and turn our minds from the world and ourselves towards him, and to beget and nourish that which is pure and living, of himself, in us; yet, notwithstanding this, there remains somewhat at first, yea, and perhaps for a long time, which is to be searched out by the light of the Lord, and brought down and subdued by his afflicting hand. When there is, indeed, somewhat of an holy will formed in the day of God's power; and the soul, in some measure, begotten and brought forth to live to God, in the heavenly wisdom; yet all the earthly will and wisdom is not thereby presently removed; but there are hidden things of the old nature and spirit, still remaining; which, perhaps, appear not, but sink inward into their root, that they may save their life; which man cannot possibly find out in his own heart, but as the Lord reveals them to him. But how doth the Lord find them out? Oh, consider! his "fire is in Zion, and his furnace is in Jerusalem." By his casting into the furnace of affliction, the fire searcheth. The deep, sore, distressing affliction, which rends and tears the very inwards, finds out both the seed and the chaff, purifying the pure gold and consuming the dross; and then, at length, the quiet state is witnessed, and the quiet fruit of righteousness brought forth, by the searching and consuming nature and operation of the fire. Oh that thy soul may be tried unto victory over all that is not of the pure life in thee! and that thou mayst wait to feel the pure seed, or measure of life in thee, and die into the seed, feeling death unto all that is not of the seed in thee! and that thou mayst feel life, healing, refreshment, support, and comfort from the God of thy life, in the seed;—and nowhere else, nor at any time, but as the Lord pleaseth to administer it to thee there. Oh, the Lord guide thee daily, and keep thy mind to him; at least, looking towards the holy place of the springing up of his life and power in thy heart. Look unto him. Help, pity, salvation, will arise in his due time; but it will not arise from any thing thou canst do or think; and faith will spring and patience be given, and hope in the tender Father of mercy, and a meek and quiet spirit will be witnessed; and the Lamb's nature springing up and opening in thee, from his precious seed, which will excel in nature, kind, degree, and virtue, all the faith, patience, hope, meekness, &c. which thou, or any else, otherwise can attain unto. Oh, look not at thy pain or sorrow, how great soever; but look from them, look off them, look beyond them, to the Deliverer! whose power is over them, and whose loving, wise, and tender Spirit is able to do thee good by them. And, if the *outward* afflictions work out an exceeding weight of glory, oh, what shall the *inward* do for those, who are humbly, brokenly, and faithfully exercised before the Lord by them! Oh, wait to feel the seed, and the cry of thy soul in the breathing life of the seed, to its Father, with its sweet, kindly, and natural subjection to him. And wait for the risings of the power in thy heart, in the Father's seasons, and for faith in the power; that thou mayst feel inward healing, of all the inward wounds which the Lord makes in thy soul, through his love to thee for thy good.

If thou wilt receive the kingdom that cannot be shaken, thou must wait to have that discovered in thee, which may be shaken; and the Lord arising terribly to shake the earth, and it removed out of its place as a cottage, and the heavens also rolled up like a scroll. And, while the Lord is doing this, he will be hiding thee in the hollow of his hand, (thy mind still retiring to the seed,) and will, in these troublesome and dismal times, inwardly be forming the new heavens and the new earth, wherein, when they are brought forth and established, dwells righteousness. The Lord lead thee, day by day, in the right way, and keep thy mind stayed upon him, in whatever befalls thee; that the belief of his love and hope in his mercy, when thou art at the lowest ebb, may keep up thy head above the billows; and that thou mayst go on in the disciple's state, learning righteousness and holiness of Him who teacheth to deny and put off unholiness and unrighteousness, and to know, embrace, and put on newness of life, and the holiness and righteousness thereof.

The Lord God of my life be with thee, preserving and ordering thy heart for the great day of his love and mercy; which will come in the appointed season, when the heart is fully exercised and fitted by the Lord for it, and will not tarry.     I. P.

## LETTER XVI.

ON BEING INGRAFTED INTO CHRIST, BEING PRESERVED ALIVE IN HIM, AND GROWING UP IN HIM IN ALL THINGS.

### To S. W.

DEAR S. W.:—

I have ever had a love to thee, and have many times been filled with earnest desires for thee; that thou mayst know the Lord in his own pure teachings, and travel into, and dwell in, the fulness of the kingdom of his dear Son; and that thou mayst be blessed with spiritual blessings in heavenly places in Christ.

In order to arrive here, thou must wait to know God and Christ, in the mystery of their Spirit, life, and power, and, by that Spirit, life, and power, find the secrets of the mystery of darkness searched and purged out, and the mystery of godliness opened and established in thy heart, in the room thereof;—Christ formed inwardly; the soul formed, yea, and created inwardly anew in him; a real transplanting into his death, and a real feeling of his springing and rising life; and an experience of the sweetness, safety, and virtue of his rising life,—and daily to be sensible what it is to lie down in the holy, quickening power, and to rise again in the risings of the life and power, and so, be only what thou art made and preserved to be, in the light, grace, life, virtue, and power of the

Lord Jesus Christ; and to feel him remove any thing that is unrighteous, and clothing thee with his pure life, Spirit, and righteousness.

Oh, this is indeed the pure, precious, living knowledge of the Lord Jesus Christ; which all the outward knowledge tends to lead to, and is comprehended and ended in. This is the excellency of the knowledge of Jesus Christ our Lord which Paul was so ravished with, and counted all things but dross and dung for. Now, that thou mayst obtain this, mind the inward appearance, the root, the fountain, the rock within, the living stone within,—its openings, its springings, its administering life to thee; and take heed of running into the outwardness of openings concerning the heavenly things, but keep, oh, learn to keep, oh, mind to keep in the inwardness of life within! This is the everlasting habitation of the birth which is begotten and brought forth, bred up and kept alive, alone by the presence, power, and operation of the living Spirit;—and the Lord Jesus is that Spirit, as really as he was man, even the holy, heavenly, immaculate spotless Lamb of God. And in this state, life reigns in the heart, and the horn of the Holy One is exalted, the head of the serpent crushed, yea, Satan trod under foot, by the God of peace,—who would have his children dwell in the sweetness and fulness of the gospel, in the peace, life, righteousness, and joy of his blessed Spirit and power.

Oh, who would not desire after, and wait for, and walk with the Lord towards the obtaining and possessing of these things? All the promises in Christ are yea and amen. Inward victory is promised; the inward presence of God is promised; God's dwelling and walking in the soul is promised; Christ supping with the soul, and the soul with him, is promised; putting the law in the heart, and writing it there; putting the pure, living fear into it; yea, also putting the holy, powerful Spirit into it, which can cause it to walk in God's ways, and to keep his righteous judgments, and do them: and He is able to do this work in the heart; for what cannot the spirit of judgment and burning consume and burn up within? Yea, all these things are promised. He can cause the soul to rejoice in the Lord, and work righteousness, and to remember the Lord in his ways, as some were taught and enabled to do in former times, Isa. lxiv. 5; yea, he can bring into the way of holiness the King of Glory's highway, into which no unclean thing can enter, and [can] keep undefiled therein; and they that are kept undefiled therein, taste the sweetness, blessedness, purity, and holy pleasure thereof.

I would fain have my own soul and thine, and all the real, serious, faithful people of God experience, and be able to say with David that which, after his many trials, afflictions, troubles, temptations, and grievous fall, he was able to say, in relation to his walking with the Lord, "For I have kept the ways of the Lord, and have not wickedly departed from my God. For all his judgments were before me, and I did not put away his statutes from me. I was also upright before him, and I kept myself from iniquity." Psa. xviii. 21, 22, 23. Oh, this is precious! when a man comes to know his iniquity, wherein the enemy's strength lies as to him, and whereby the enemy hath most advantage to tempt and gain ground on him, brought down and subdued. Certainly, when one gains strength from God to overcome the enemy here, and to keep out of this, he comes very near to the keeping of himself, in and by virtue of the Holy Spirit and power, so as the wicked one cannot touch him, nor draw him to touch any unclean thing. If that be indeed put off wherein the enemy's power lies, and that indeed put on wherein the strength of the Lord Jesus is revealed, and the soul be really in the possession of and abide in this state, how can it but be strong in the Lord, and in the power of his might, and witness the good pleasure of the goodness of the Lord fulfilling, and the work of faith going on with power, daily more and more; a little measure whereof, kept to, removes the mountains inwardly and gives strength over the enemy. How then doth it increase and grow up in life and virtue, and in a sensible understanding and experience of the name of the Lord Jesus! Is there not in this state a feeling of remission of sins, a feeling of redemption, a feeling of reconciliation, a feeling of oneness with God in Christ, a feeling of God being the salvation, strength, and song, and a trusting in him, and not being afraid? Isa. xii. 2. Is there not a being careful in nothing, but in every thing making the requests to God, by prayer and supplication, with thanksgiving, in that Spirit and holy breath of life which the Father cannot deny, and so, the peace of God, which passeth all understanding, keeping the heart and mind through Christ Jesus?

Oh, my friend, there is an ingrafting into Christ,—a being formed and new-created in Christ,—a living and abiding in him, and a growing and bringing forth fruit through him unto perfection. Oh, mayest thou experience all these things! and, that thou mayest so do, wait to know life, the springings of life, the separations of life inwardly from all that evil which hangs about it, and would be springing up and mixing with it, under an appearance of good; that life may come to live fully in thee, and nothing else. And so, sink very low, and become very little, and know little; yea, know no power to believe, act, or suffer any thing for God, but as it is given thee, by the springing grace, virtue, and life of the Lord Jesus. For grace is a spiritual, inward thing, and holy seed sown by God, springing up in the heart. People have got a notion of grace, but know not the thing. Do not thou matter the notion, but feel the thing, and know thy heart more and more ploughed up by the Lord, that his seed's grace may grow up in thee more and more, and thou mayest daily feel thy heart as a garden, more and more enclosed, watered, dressed, and delighted in by him.

This is a salutation of love from thy friend in the Truth, which lives and changes not.     I. P.

27th of Twelfth Month, 1678.

---

## LETTER XVII.

#### COUNSEL TO ONE TOSSED AS WITH TEMPESTS.

Dear Friend:—

Thy condition cannot but be weak and dark, until the light of life arise in thee, and the power of the Lord overcome and subdue the power of darkness, which strives to keep the seed of life in the grave and bonds of death.

It is the Lord's mercy, to give thee breathings after life and cries unto him against that which oppresseth thee; and happy wilt thou be, when he shall fill thy soul with that which he hath given thee to breathe after. Only let thy heart wait for strength to trust him with the season, for his long-tarrying is thy salvation, and the destruction of those enemies which, while any strength remains in them, will never suffer thee and thy God to dwell uninterruptedly together. Therefore they must needs die, and He who hath the power to kill them knows the way, which, to the appearing of thy sense, will be as if he meant to kill the life of *thy soul*, and not *them*. But lie still under his hand, and be content to be unable to judge concerning his ways and workings in thy heart; and thou shalt at times feel an inward leaven of life from his Holy Spirit, whereby he will change and transform thy spirit into his likeness, in some measure, for the present. And though it be quickly gone again, and the whole land so overspread with enemies that there is no sight of redemption or the Redeemer left, but the soul in a worse condition than before,—yet be not troubled,—for if troubles abound, and there be tossing, and storms, and tempests, and no peace, nor any thing visible left to support, yet lie still, and sink beneath till a secret hope stir, which will stay the heart in the midst of all these,—until the Lord administer comfort, who knows how and what relief to give to the weary traveller, that knows not where it is, nor which way to look, nor where to expect a path.

How shall I speak to thee, how shall I mourn over thee? Oh that thou mayest be upheld to the day of God's mercy to thy soul! and be gathered out of all such knowledge, as thou canst comprehend or contain in what is natural, into the feeling of life; that thou mayest know the difference between living upon somewhat received from God, and having God live with thee and administer life to thee at his pleasure; thou being kept in the nothingness, emptiness, poverty, and perfect resignation of spirit.

This counsel is to thee, through a poor, weak vessel

I. P.

## LETTER XVIII.

#### ENCOURAGEMENT UNDER TRIALS INCIDENT TO BEARING THE CROSS OF CHRIST.

Who is able to undergo the crosses and afflictions, either inward or outward, which befall those, whom God draws out of the spirit of this world and path of destruction, into the way of eternal rest and peace? Yet the Lord is able to uphold that which feels its weakness, and daily waits on him for support, under the heaviness of the cross.

I know, dear heart, thy outward trials cannot but be sharp and bitter; and I know also that the Lord is able to sustain thee under him, and cause thee to stand thy ground; that thou give not advantage to that spirit, which hereby would draw from the Lord, and from the way of life and happiness. Oh that thou couldst dwell in the knowledge and sense of this! even that the Lord beholds thy sufferings with an eye of pity, and is able, not only to uphold thee under them, but also to do thee good by them, and to bring forth that life and wisdom in thee by means thereof, to which he will give dominion over that spirit which grieves and afflicts thee, in his due season. Therefore grieve not at thy lot, be not discontented, look not out at the hardness of thy condition; but when the storm and matters of vexation are sharp, look up to Him who can give meekness and patience, can lift up thy head over all, and cause thy life to grow, and be a gainer by all. If the Lord God did not help us by his mighty arm, how often should we fall and perish! and if the Lord God help thee proportionably to thy condition of affliction and distress, thou wilt have no cause to complain, but to bless his name. He is exceedingly good, and gracious, and tender-hearted, and doth not despise the afflictions of the afflicted, for his name's sake, in any kind.

This is in tender love towards thee, with breathings to my Father, that his pleasant plant may not be crushed in thee by the foot of pride and violence, but may overgrow it, and flourish the more because of it.

From thy truly loving friend in the Truth, and for the Truth's sake,                         I. P.

## LETTER XIX.

### ON BEING OFFENDED WITH THOSE WHO FALL INTO TEMPTATION.

It is of the infinite mercy and compassion of the Lord, that his pure love visiteth any of us; and it is by the preservation thereof alone that we stand. If he leave us at any time, but one moment, what are we? and who is there that provoketh him not to depart? Let *him* throw the first stone at him that falls.

In the Truth itself, in the living power and virtue, there is no offence; but that part which is not perfectly redeemed hath still matter for the temptation to work upon, and may be taken in the snare. Let him that stands take heed lest he fall, and, in the bowels of pity, mourn over and wait for the restoring of him that is fallen. That which is so apt to be offended is the same with that which falls. Oh, do not reason, in the high-mindedness, against any that turn aside from the pure Guide; but fear lest the unbelieving and fleshly wise part get up in thee also. Oh, know the weakness of the creature in the withdrawings of the life! and the strength of the enemy in that hour! and the free grace and mercy which alone can preserve! and thou wilt rather wonder that *any* stand, than that *some* fall.

When the pure springs of life open in the heart, immediately the enemy watcheth his opportunity to get entrance, and many times finds entrance soon after, the soul little fearing or suspecting him, having lately felt such mighty, unconquerable strength; and yet, how often then doth he get in, and smite the life down to the ground! and what may he not do with the creature, unless the Lord graciously help!

Oh, great is the mystery of godliness, the way of life narrow, the travel to the land of rest long, hard, and sharp; it is easy miscarrying, it is easy stepping aside, at any time, it is easy losing the Lord's glorious presence, unless the defence about it, by his Almighty arm, be kept up. There is a time for the Lord's taking down the fence of his own vineyard, because of transgression, and then the wild boar may easily break in. Ah! who tastes not of this, in some measure? and what hinders that he taste not of it in a greater measure?

Ah! turn from the fleshly wisdom and reasonings unto the pure river of life itself; and wait there, to have that judged which hath taken offence; lest, if it grow stronger in thee, it draw thee from the life, which alone is able to preserve thee, and so thou also fall!

This is in dear love to thee: retire from that part which looketh out, and feel the inward virtue of that which can restore and preserve thee.     I. P.

---

## LETTER XX.

### ON SHUNNING THE CROSS.

*To Catharine Pordage.*

AH, my poor, distressed, entangled friend:—

While thou seekest to avoid the snare, thou deeply runnest into it; for thou art feeding on the tree of knowledge in giving way to these thoughts, reasonings, and suggestions, which keep thee from obedience to that which hath been made manifest to thy understanding. And thou mayest well be feeble in thy mind while thou art thus separated from Him who is thy strength, and lettest in his enemy. This is not the right feebleness of mind which God pities, not the right way of waiting to receive strength. Why shouldst not thou act so far as God gives thee light? and why shouldst thou not appear willing to obey him, even in little things, so far as he hath given thee light? What if I should say, that all this is but the subtlety of the serpent's wisdom to avoid the cross, and is not that simplicity and plainness of heart towards God which thou takest it to be; and that thou art loath to be so poor, and low, and mean in the eyes of others, as this practice would make thee appear?

Thy friend in the Truth, and in sincere love.

I. P.

AMERSHAM, 25th of Ninth Month, 1675.

---

## LETTER XXI.

ON LOVE, MEEKNESS, AND WATCHING OVER EACH OTHER.

*To Friends in Amersham.*

FRIENDS :—

Our life is love, and peace, and tenderness, and bearing one with another, and forgiving one another, and not laying accusations one against another; but praying one for another, and helping one another up with a tender hand, if there has been any slip or fall, and waiting till the Lord gives sense and repentance, if sense and repentance in any be wanting. Oh, wait to feel this spirit, and to be guided to walk in this spirit, that ye may enjoy the Lord in sweetness, and walk sweetly, meekly, tenderly, peaceably, and lovingly one with another. And then ye will be a praise to the Lord; and any thing that is, or hath been, or may be amiss, ye will come over in the true dominion, even in the Lamb's dominion; and that which is contrary shall be trampled upon, as life rises and rules in you. So, watch your hearts and ways; and watch one over another in that which is gentle and tender, and knows it can neither preserve itself nor help another out of the snare; but the Lord must be waited upon to do this in and for us all. So, mind Truth, the service, enjoyment, and possession of it in your hearts; and so to walk as ye may bring no disgrace upon it, but may be a good savor in the places where ye live: the meek, innocent, tender, righteous life reigning in you, governing over you, and shining through you, in the eyes of all with whom ye converse.

Your friend in the Truth, and a desirer of your welfare and prosperity therein.     I. P.

AYLESBURY, 4th of Third Month, 1667.

## LETTER XXII.

### ON THE SPIRITUAL APPEARANCE OF CHRIST.

O Friend!—

That thou hadst the true sense of the drift of my heart in writing and sending things to thee: which is and hath been this,—that thou mightst be acquainted with that of God in the heart, which quickens to him; and, in the light of that, mightst try thy heart and ways, and so, only justify in thyself what God justifies, and let all else go.

Shall the Lord appear mightily on the earth, and Israel not know him? Shall the professors of this age understand no more his appearance in Spirit than the Jews did his appearance in flesh? Shall they stumble at the very same stumbling-stone? Yes, the same stumbling-stone is laid for that wisdom to stumble at, as in all generations; and there is no avoiding stumbling but by coming out of that wisdom into babelike simplicity, which gives entrance into pure, heavenly wisdom. And this I dare affirm, as in God's presence and in his pure fear, having received the sense thereof from him,—that there is none that opposeth this his present appearance, (by the greatest knowledge and wisdom of their comprehensions from the letter,) but would also have opposed and denied his appearance in that body of flesh had they lived in that day. For the wisdom which *they* gathered from the letter did not reveal Christ in *that day*, but the Father; and the same reveals him in *this* day.

Oh that thou couldst feel the pure revelation from the Father to thy heart! Oh, wait for a new heart, a new ear, a new eye! even to feel the pure in thee, and thy mind changed by the pure, that all things may become new to thee,—the Scriptures new, (they are so, indeed, when God opens them,) duties new, ordinances new, graces new, experiences new, a new church of the Spirit's building, wherein He and thy soul may dwell together, and thou mayst be able to say, in the presence of the Lord, This is a city of God's own building, the foundation whereof is laid with sapphires, whose walls are salvation, and its gates praise! I. P.

12th of Third Month, 1669.

## LETTER XXIII.

### TO ONE UNDER DIVINE VISITATION.

Oh, dear Friend!—

The eternal love of my Father is to thee; and because he loves thee and would entirely enjoy thee, therefore doth he so grievously batter and break down that which stands in the way. What he is doing towards thee thou canst not know now, but thou shalt know hereafter. Only be still, and wait for the springing up of hope in the seasons the Father sees necessary, that thou mayst not faint under his hand, but be supported by his secret power, until his work be finished. The great thing necessary for thee at present to know is the drawings of his Spirit, that thou mayst not ignorantly withstand or neglect them, and protract the day of thy redemption.

Oh, look not after great things! small breathings, small desires, after the Lord, if true and pure, are sweet beginnings of life. Take heed of despising "the day of small things," by looking after some great visitation, proportionable to thy distress, according to thy eye. Nay, thou must become a child, thou must lose thy own will quite by degrees. Thou must wait for life to be measured out by the Father, and be content with what proportion, and at what time, he shall please to measure.

Oh, be little, be little! and then thou wilt be content with little: and if thou feel, now and then, a check or a secret smiting, in *that* is the Father's love: be not over-wise, nor over-eager, in thy own willing, running, and desiring, and thou mayst feel it so, and by degrees come to the knowledge of thy Guide, who will lead thee, step by step, in the path of life, and teach thee to follow and, in his own season, powerfully judge that which cannot, nor will not, follow. Be still, and wait for light and strength: and desire not to know or comprehend, but to be known and comprehended in the love and life which seeks out, gathers, and preserves the lost sheep.

I remain thy dear friend and a well-wisher to thy soul, in the love of my Father.   I. P.

---

## LETTER XXIV.

ENCOURAGEMENT TO LOOK UP TO THE LORD AMIDST HIS CHASTENINGS, AND THE SMITINGS OF THE ENEMY.

Friend :—

Thy advantage in thy travels is great over what it hath been; the Lord having given thee a better sight, both of thy enemies and of that wherein his strength against them is revealed.

Now, what remains but that thou hope in him, and breathe unto him, and hang upon him, that his virtue may flow into thee, and the mountains and difficulties may pass away before the presence of the Seed who is revealed in thee?

Look down no more, look out no more, but dwell with thy Beloved in the tent that he hath pitched for thee. Let him do what he will, let him appear how he will, wait on him in the daily exercise; stand still in the faith and see him working out thy salvation, and scattering the bones of them that have besieged thee. Think not hardly of him by no means; question not his carrying on of his work. He knows what yet he hath to do, and what stratagem the enemy yet hath to surprise and entangle thee. Oh, feel his arm stretched out for thee! and be not so much discouraged in the sight of what is yet to be done, as comforted in his good-will towards thee! 'Tis true he hath chastened thee with rods and sore afflictions, but did he ever take away his loving-kindness from thee? or did his faithfulness ever fail in the sorest, blackest, thickest, darkest night that ever befell thee? And breathe to him for the carrying on of his work, that thou mayst feel his presence and life getting dominion over death daily in thee, more and more. And wait to feel strength of life, that thy growth may be pure, and the holy seed may have dominion and be all in thee. I. P.

8th of the Eighth Month, 1666.

### POSTSCRIPT.

The enemy will be laying snares and forging subtle devices to darken and bow thee down, which (thou, not being hasty to believe, join with, and let in as true, but waiting on the Lord in singleness, fear, and humility) his light will spring up in thee and help thee to discern. And, oh, how sweet will it be for thee, who has so often been ensnared, to escape the gins and nets of the fowler, and to dwell in the rest and peace which thy soul hath tasted of, and which is the proper place of thy habitation!

Indeed, the Lord's thoughts have not been towards thee as thou hast apprehended all along. His angel was towards the enemy, towards the oppressor, not towards thee. Nor doth he judge and smite the mind after that manner that the enemy doth accuse, but according to his own nature, sweetness, and tender love. And his judgments and smiting have other effects than the serpent's accusings and piercings, for *they* do not drive *from* him, but they melt, and tender, and prepare the heart for union with him. Oh, keep close to the measure of life, wherein thou mayst discern and distinguish these things; and take heed of letting in one bowing-down thought, (how manifest or demonstrative soever,) but look up to him who hath freely loved and hath abounded in mercy towards thee, that, in the faith, patience, stillness, and meekness of his seed, thou mayst be found always waiting upon him in the several exercises wherewith he shall daily see good to exercise thee, till he bring forth his seed in dominion in thee, and thereby give thee thy desired and expected end.

I. P.

9th of the Eighth Month, 1666.

## LETTER XXV.

### ON UNRESERVED OBEDIENCE.

*To Bridget Atley.*

Dear Friend:—

I know thy soul desires to live; and my soul desires that thou mightst live. Oh, why art thou so backward to hearken to the voice which is nigh thee, wherein is life? why dost thou reason? why dost thou consult? why dost thou expect? why dost thou hope? why dost thou believe against thy own soul?

The snares of the subtle one will entangle forever, unless thou wait for, hearken to, and obey the voice of the living God, who leads thee single-hearted and obedient out of them. Is there any way of life but one? Is not the Lord leading his children in that way? Must not all that come after follow in the footsteps of those that go before? Is there any Saviour, but the seed of life and the Father of it? Is it not the same in thee as in others? Hath it not the same voice? Oh that thou hadst the same ear and the same heart, that thou mightst hear, receive, and live! They wait aright: dost thou wait so? they hope aright: dost thou hope so? If not, what will thy waiting and expecting come to? In *that*, which hath sometimes inclined thy heart, *there* is Truth, *there* were the beginnings of salvation; but in *that*, which draws thee out, to expect some great matters, and dries up thy present sense, and hinders thy present subjection, *therein* is deceit and the destruction of thy soul. Therefore, if thou desire and love the salvation thereof, oh, hasten, hasten out of it! wait for the reproofs of wisdom; and what it manifests to be of the earthly and worldly nature in thee, (the words, ways, thoughts, customs thereof,) hasten out of. Oh, turn thy back upon the world with speed, and turn thy face towards the heavenly wisdom and light eternal! which will be springing up in thee, if thou turn thy back upon the world and wait for it.

And do not look for such great matters to begin with; but be content to be a child, and let the Father proportion out daily to thee what light, what power, what exercises, what straits, what fears, what troubles, he sees fit for thee; and do thou bow before him continually, in humility of heart, who hath the disposal of thee, whether to life or death forever. Ah! that wisdom which would be choosing must be confounded, and the low humble thing raised, which submits, and cries to the Father in every condition. And in waiting to feel *this,* and in joining to *this,* thou mayest meet with life; but death, destruction, and separation from God is the portion of the *other* forever! Oh that thou mayst be separated from it, and joined to the seed and birth of God! that in it thy soul may spring up to know, serve, and worship the Lord, and to wait daily to be formed by him, until thou become perfectly like him! But thou must join in with the beginnings of life, and be exercised with the day of small things, before thou meet with great things, wherein is the clearness and satisfaction of the soul. The rest is at noonday; but the travels begin at the breakings of day, wherein are but glimmerings, or little light, wherein the discovery of good and evil are not so manifest and certain, yet *there* must the traveller begin to travel, and in his faithful travels (in much fear and trembling, lest he should err) the light will break in upon him more and more.

This have I written in tenderness to thee, that thou mightest not miss of the path of the living, which is appointed of the Father to lead, and alone can lead, the soul to life. Oh that thou mightest be enlightened and quickened by the Lord to walk therein, and mightst be thankful for, and content with, what he gives thee, and walk therein, from the evil to the good, from the earthly to the heavenly nature daily, and mightst not despise the cross or the shame of the seed! For I know there is a wisdom in thee, which will despise and turn from it, until the Lord batter and crucify it; and I can hardly put up a more proper request for thee, than that the Lord would draw out his sword against it, and deeply perplex and confound it in thee. I. P.

1665.

## LETTER XXVI.

#### AFFLICTIONS MAY WORK OUT A WEIGHT OF GLORY.

*To my dear suffering Friends in Scotland.*

DEAR FRIENDS AND BRETHREN :—
Who have partaken of the tender mercy and blessed visitation of the Lord.

Oh, blessed be the Lord who pitied and helped us in our low estate, and whose tender love and mercy hath followed us from his first visiting us to this present day! And indeed the Lord is with us, (what can we desire more?) preparing us for himself, preserving us in the life of his blessed Truth, building us up more and more, and causing his Spirit of glory and living power to rest upon us, and the virtue thereof to spring up in us day by day.

Oh, the beauty and glory of the day of our God increaseth upon his heritage, blessed be the name of the Lord! And to what tend all the workings of the contrary spirit and power but to eat out its own interest and kingdom through the Lord's blessed ordering of things, so that all things work together for good and for the advancing of Truth, and the growth of it in the hearts of God's heritage?

So, my dear friends, none look out, either at outward or inward sufferings, but to the Lord only, whose life, Spirit, and power is above them, and bears up all over them who are in Spirit joined to him, faithfully waiting upon him, which God daily teaches and enables his to do. Thus, my dear friends, feel the Lord's presence and power among you, who is always near his, but especially in the time of their straits, trials, and sufferings; and wait to feel the life springing and doing its proper work in each of you day by day; working out what is to be wrought out in any, and working more and more into the glory of the heavenly image, that, through the sufferings, ye may come into the glory, and be crowned with the glory, virtue, holiness, righteousness, and dominion of life over all; and thus, the Son may sit upon his throne in you, and wield his holy and righteous sceptre, and give you dominion in and with him over all that would veil life, or keep it under, in any of you. So, my dear friends, be strong in the Lord, with the strength of the Lord, with which he is clothing those whom he hath emptied and made weak; for the trials, temptations, and afflictions, prepare for, and (as I may say) lead into the possession of the desired inheritance, where all that the soul hath breathed and waited for is bestowed upon it by the bountiful hand of the Father of mercies, who keeps covenant and mercy forever, and renews covenant and mercy day by day.

So the tender God of my life and Father of the blessings and mercies of my once greatly distressed and miserable soul, instruct you, preserve you, watch over you, exercise your spirits most advantageously, daily open you to himself, keep you empty and naked before him of all your own clothing and righteousness, and fill you with that which flows from the pure living fountain, to the unspeakable joy of your hearts and the glory of his own name over all forever!

Be of good faith, my dear friends, look not out at any thing, fear none of those things ye may be exposed to suffer, either outwardly or inwardly, but trust the Lord over all, and your life will spring, and grow, and refresh you, and the love and power will purge out, and keep out, what would hinder its growth; and ye will learn obedience and faithfulness daily more and more, even by your exercises and sufferings; yea, the Lord will teach you the very mystery of faith and obedience, (oh, blessed lesson!) and ye shall not be disappointed of your hope or crown by any thing the enemy can plot or bring about against you, but have the weight of glory increased and enlarged by his temptations and your many sufferings; the wisdom, power, love, and goodness of the Lord ordering *every* thing for you, and ordering *your* hearts in every thing,—you having given up to him, and keeping them continually given up to him, in the holy seed of Truth, in which he hath in some measure already joined, and is daily more and more joining you to himself.

This is the salutation and tender visit of the love of your brother in the Truth, whose breathings are to God for you, and his praises unto Him, through the sense of his being with you, and daily showing mercy to you, upholding and preserving you in the midst of your sore trials and afflictions.     I. P.

LONDON, 5th of Fifth Month, 1676.

---

## LETTER XXVII.

### AN INVITATION TO HEAVENLY SUBSTANCE.

FRIEND:—

The vessel, or created nature, poisoned by sin and death, nothing can redeem, but the life and power of God revealed in the vessel. This life, this peace, this power, this righteousness, this salvation, is the Lord Jesus Christ. And he that feels any thing of this feels somewhat of Christ; and, being joined to and partaking of it, partakes somewhat of his redemption; for it is not by an outward knowledge, but by an inward virtue and spiritual life, received from Christ, and held in Christ, that those who are saved are saved. This is the thing of value with me, for which I have been made willing to part with all, and into this purchased possession am I daily travelling; and, in my travels, the Father of life and tender mercy pleaseth to help me.

Now, to have thee gathered into this light, this life, this power, which is of Christ, and in which he is and appears, is the desire of my soul, in uprightness of heart before the Lord, for thee: and, if he please, I am willing to be instrumental in his hand towards the bringing forth of this in thee. It is not my desire to bring forth new notions in thee, but rather that thou mightst wait on the Lord, for him to bring up his living, powerful Truth in thee, wherein the knowledge of the new and living way is alone revealed.

I am a worm, I am poor, I am nothing, less than nothing, as in myself, weaker than I can express, or thou imagine; yet in the midst of all this, the life, power, righteousness, and presence of Christ is my refreshment, peace, joy, and crown: and that to which I invite thee is substance, everlasting substance, which thou shalt know and acknowledge in spirit to be so, as that is created and raised in thee which can see and acknowledge it in Truth. Oh, wait on the Lord, fear before him, pray for his fear in the upright breathings, (which are not of thy spirit's forming, but of his pure begetting,) that thou mayest be led by him out of that wisdom which entangles into that innocency, simplicity, and precious childishness in which the Father appears to the soul to break the bonds and snares of iniquity; for, hereby, the evil spirit not only involveth in iniquity, but also begets a belief, as if there could be no perfect redemption therefrom till the time of redemption be over.

Thy truly loving friend, desiring the right guidance and happiness of thy soul by the Lord Jesus Christ, the alone skilful Shepherd and Guide, even as of my own soul. I. P.

AYLESBURY PRISON,
20th of Tenth Month, 1666.

---

## LETTER XXVIII.

### ADVICE RESPECTING CHURCH DISCIPLINE.

*To the Women's Meeting of Friends in the Truth, at John Mannock's.*

DEAR FRIENDS:—

Dearly beloved and honored in the Lord, because of his honorable presence and power, which is so preciously manifested and found to be among you in your meetings.

Blessed be the Lord, who hath thus gathered you, and given you hearts to meet together, to feel his precious presence and power, and wait to do his will therein, as he shall please to call, and make your way clear thereto. And blessed be the Lord, who doth encourage and reward you daily, and make your meetings pleasant and advantageous to your own souls, and towards the seasoning and holy watching over the several respective places where your lot is fallen.

Oh, what could the Lord do more for his people than to turn them to that pure seed of life which will make them all alive, and keep them all in life and purity, and then to make use of every living member in the living body, as his Spirit shall please to breathe upon it, and his power actuate it! And, indeed, there is need of all the life and power to the body which the Lord sees good to bestow on any member of it,—every member of the body having life given it, not only for itself, but likewise for the use and service of the body. Only, dear friends, here is to be the great care, that every member keep within the limits of life, wherein its capacity and ability for service lies, and out of which it can do no real service for God, or to the body. Oh, therefore, eye life, eye the power, eye the presence of the Lord with your spirits, that he may go along with you, and guide you in every thought ye think, in every word ye speak, in reference to his work and service.

And mind, friends, what is now upon me to you: it is one thing to sit waiting to feel the power, and to keep within the limits of the power, thus far; and another, yea, and harder, to feel and keep within the sense and limits of the power when ye come to act. Then your reasonings, your wisdom, your apprehensions have more advantage to get up in you and to put themselves forth. Oh, therefore, watch narrowly and diligently against the forward part, and keep back to the life, which, though it rise more slowly, yet acts more surely and safely for God.

Oh, wait and watch, to feel your Keeper keeping you within the holy bounds and limits, within the pure fear, within the living sense, while ye are acting for your God,—that ye may only be his instruments, and feel him acting in you. Therefore, every one wait to feel the Judge risen and up, and the judgment set in your own hearts, that what ariseth in you may be judged, and nothing may pass away from you publicly but what hath first passed the pure judgment in your own breasts; and let the holy rule of the blessed apostle James be always upon your spirits:— "Let every one be swift to hear, slow to speak, slow to wrath." Oh, let not a talkativeness have place in any of you, but abide in such gravity, modesty, and weightiness of spirit as becomes the judgment-seat of the Spirit and power of the Lord! Ye can never wait too much for the power, nor can ye ever act too much in the power; but ye may easily act too much without it.

And as for this troublesome, contentious business, (if the Lord should yet order it to be brought before you,) the Lord teach you to consider of and manage it in a wise, tender, and healing spirit! Ye must distinguish in judgment, if ye judge aright, between enemies and erring friends. And take heed of the quickness and strength of reason,—or of the natural part,—which avails little; but wait for the evidence and demonstration of God's Spirit, which reaches to the witness, and doth the work. Are they in a snare? are they overtaken in a fault? yea, are they in measure blinded and hardened so that they can neither see nor feel as to this particular? Retire, sit still a while, and travail for them. Feel how life will arise in any of you, and how mercy will reach towards them; and how living words, from the tender sense, may be reached forth to their hearts, deeply, by the hand of the Lord, for their good. And, if ye find them at length bowing to the Lord, oh, let tender compassion help them forwards, that what hath been so troublesome and groundedly dissatisfactory in the progress may at length have a sweet issue for their good, and our joy and rejoicing in the Lord!

So, my dear friends, the Lord be with you and guide you in this and in all that he shall further call you to, and multiply his presence, power, and blessings upon you, and make your meetings as serviceable to the honor of his name as he himself would have them, and as you yourselves can desire them to be.

Your friend and brother in the tender Truth, and in the pure love and precious life.    I. P.

19th of Fifth Month, 1678.

## LETTER XXIX.

OF PRESERVATION AND A GROWTH IN THE HEAVENLY LIFE; ITS POWER OVER THE EARTHLY NATURE.

*To the single, upright-hearted, and faithful friends of Truth in and about the two Chalfonts.*

DEAR FRIENDS:—

Have ye in any measure drunk in the sense of what the Lord hath done for you? and have ye felt meltings of spirit, and bowings before him, with praises to his name therefor? Indeed, my request is to the Lord for you, that he would please to keep you truly sensible of what he already is to you, and of what he hath already done for you; that he would also, of his tender mercy and great goodness, visit you yet further, increase life in you, cause faith to abound, give you to dwell in his power, and always abide in his seed, and feel *that* to be your hope, peace, joy, life, and strength, continually,—that ye may more and more give thanks unto him, as ye feel his pure life arising in you, and death and the grave swallowed up thereby.

Ah, my friends, can we ever forget the lost and miserable estate wherein the mercy of the Lord and his power from on high visited us? Oh, the blackness of that day, the misery, the deep distress of that day, which some of your souls felt! Did ye not know what it was to want God, and to lie open to the furious assaults of the enemy, when ye felt no strength nor knew whither to retire to keep out any hurt, any temptation, any vain thought and imagination, or to give you any grounded hope in the goodness and mercy of the Lord? How did ye mourn, how did ye cry out and pine away in your iniquities day and night, and knew not which way to look, nor what to wait for! Are there not among you who have known this state and felt somewhat of that which I now relate? Sure I am, there are upon the earth who can witness it to the full, whose mouths and hearts are now filled with a sense of the Lord's goodness and of his great salvation, and with deep and high praises to his name.

But, my dear friends, is there any of you (I know to whom I speak, even to the sensible, to the diligent, to the faithful among you) who cannot in truth witness, as in God's presence, concerning the arm and power of his salvation which ye have often felt? insomuch that ye can sing that song, "He hath raised up an horn of salvation for us in the house of his servant David; as he spake by the mouth of his holy prophets." Do ye not know the house of his servant David with the horn of salvation in it, and that horn raised up to you for your defence and comfort? Yea, do ye not daily feel the Lord ministering out salvation to you from it? Are not your enemies daily overcome by the faith which he hath given you in his power? May I not say to you, Where is the strength of the tempter? Have ye not felt the seed of the woman to bruise the head of the serpent?

so that, in the fear of the Lord, and in the strength, virtue, and dominion of his life manifested in you, ye can say, though as yet somewhat tremblingly, **Where are those temptations, those lusts, vain thoughts, and imaginations, which once I was overcome by and overrun with?** Surely, **I may speak thus; for I know assuredly,** that the power **of the** Lord God, as it is lifted **up** in any of you, scatters these, and gives you dominion over them. For the life and its power is given as a bulwark and weapon of war against iniquity and its power; and, where it is received, it opposeth, warreth, striveth, until it **overcome.**

And this is that which gives **the victory and** overcoming,—to **wit,** faith in the seed. **The** seed felt the soul joined to it, faith in it and from it given to **the soul.** Then it becomes the Leader, **the** mighty undertaker, for the soul, and overcomes its snares and enemies for it; and, when it hath overcome them, they are overcome indeed. And then the soul lies down in peace, dwells in peace, feeds on the living nourishment in the green pastures of life in peace. Then Jerusalem, the building of life in the heart, becomes a quiet habitation where God and the soul dwell sweetly together, and there is nothing that hath **power in it to disturb, annoy, or make** afraid. Why so? Because the Lord God of power is present there, **stretcheth out his wings there, is a** pillar of cloud by **day, and a pillar of fire** by night, there. He hath raised up his glorious life in that heart whereof he is very choice, and he hath also spread a defence over his glory, with which the soul is so encompassed and defended that it feels the walls of this city to be salvation, and its gates praise.

Oh, my soul, travel on! Oh, dear friends, do ye also travel on into the fulness of the glory of this state! There is no other thing to be desired and waited for. This is your portion, both here in this world and forever. Therefore, wait in the seed of *this* life, wait to feel yet a further gathering into it, and a growing up in it, and give yourselves up to it that it may overspread and cover you. And the Lord God of life daily open it and manifest it more and more in you and to you, that ye may be more found in him, and yet more acceptable and pleasing in the eyes of your God; and may sing praises unto him, not only at the foot of the hill in some true proportion and measure of his life, but in the very heights of Zion, even in the fulness of the measure of your stature in Christ, which ye are all diligently to press after till ye arrive at. And then there is no more to be done but to spread abroad into, and drink in of, and live in the full pleasure and safety of life forever. Then may ye eat freely of the tree of life, which is in the midst of the paradise of God, and draw water with joy out of the wells of salvation!

Therefore feel, oh, feel, in spirit, the mark of the high calling of God in Christ Jesus! and be daily looking up to that which quickens to God and keeps fresh and lively in him, that none of you grow slothful, drowsy, or negligent, and so, unfaithful in relation to the great talent which God hath put into your hands; and so the Lord be provoked against you and suffer the enemy to tempt and prevail upon you; that a veil come over your hearts again, and the air thicken, and the earthly nature cover the seed, and he that hath power in that earth and over that air, captivate, **oppress, entangle, and lead you** back from God again. **Oh, cry to the Lord to keep the** eye open, and the **heart single, and the soul in the** true sense and feeling, that the heavenly voice which drew you out of the earth may be daily heard further instructing you and gathering you more and more up into him who is your life! So ye that fear the Lord and love his name, and have tasted of his goodness and powerful salvation, oh, hate evil! All that his light hath **made** manifest and drawn you from, oh, take heed **of ever dallying with again!** Oh, **never hearken to the tempter, but** pray to the Father, **that ye may** discern his baits, **and at** no time consult or reason **with him, but still wait in** every thing to feel the motion, guidance, quickening, and sweet, pure, heavenly leading of the Spirit of your Father!

Hath the Lord spoken peace to you, peace which passeth man's understanding and only flows from him? hath he given you any proportion of this precious peace? Oh, may he watch over you, and preserve you in that wisdom, **in** those heavenly instructions, in that heavenly life, divine power, and holy conversation, **wherein ye met with** that peace, and wherein alone ye can enjoy and possess it; and keep you out of all manner of sin, lust, and foolishness, of the fleshly mind and spirit; for the peace is not there. That is the fruit of the enemy to your peace, and it hath of his nature in it; it always breaks your peace, and sows distance, difference, and division, between the Giver and Maker of your peace and you. Do ye not always (ye that are in the true sense and have received the holy understanding) feel it thus, and know it to be thus? it is an eternal truth, and the eternal eye, wherever it is opened, witnesseth and sealeth to it. Therefore this little thing, this light of God in you, to which ye were at first directed and turned, which discovers all the darkness of the enemy, and all his deceits and devices, and keeps the minds of those that are stayed by it: in this wait, to this let your minds be still turned, and in it still abide, and the power and glory of eternal life will daily more and more appear in you; yea, flow and break in upon you, to the filling of your vessels with its virtue, and the causing of your hearts to abound with joy before the Lord, and with thanksgivings to him.

May the God of tender mercies and everlasting compassions cause the bowels of his love to be daily yearning towards you, that you may be nursed up with the living food, and that which would overturn and destroy his work may be opposed; that ye may feel it daily go on, yea, mightily preserved and carried on by him even till it be finished and the top stone laid, and your souls, in the true and full sense of life, cry, *Grace, grace,* to him that laid the foundation, raised up, defended, and carried on the building, and now at length hath perfected it. And thus, whatsoever ye have hitherto witnessed in measure, ye shall then witness in fulness, and see that all the promises of God are of a precious nature, and are "yea and amen" from God to the seed.

May the life, presence, and power of the Lord be with you in this seed, in your breathings after it, in your joinings to it, in your abidings and waitings upon him in it; and the Lord God give you to breathe after it, give you to join to it, give you to abide always, and wait upon him in it, and never to hearken to and go out after a contrary spirit and wisdom, but keep you in the simplicity, lowliness, humility, and tender spirit which is in Christ Jesus, to the praise of his own name, and preservation and joy of your hearts before him forever. amen.

Written in the tender bowels and motion of the pure life, from the place of my confinement in Aylesbury.

I. P.

1st of Third Month, 1667.

## LETTER XXX.

ON TRUE, LIVING, HEAVENLY KNOWLEDGE.

*To the Lady Conway.*

Dear Friend :—

I have heard both of thy love to Truth, and of thy great afflictions outwardly; both which occasion a sense concerning thee, and breathings to the tender Father of my life for thee; that thy heart may know and be joined to the Truth, and thou mayest live and walk in it, reaping the sweet comfort, support, and satisfaction which God daily ministers in and through it to his gathered and preserved ones. I am satisfied thou hast need of comforts and support: oh that thou mayest be led thither, and be daily found by the Lord there, where the comforter doth daily delight to supply the afflicted and suffering ones, whether inwardly or outwardly, with comfort.

And, my dear friend, take heed of that wisdom and knowledge which is not of the seed, and which can be held in the mind without the springing life of the seed. The first day I was convinced, I was not only convinced in my understanding concerning the seed, but I felt the seed in my heart, and my heart was enraptured with the sense and feeling of it, and my great cry to the Lord was that I might faithfully travel through all the sufferings and death of the other part, into union with an enjoyment of it; and that that wisdom which was not of the pure living root and nature might die in me. Now, how I have been exercised and taught since is hard for me to utter. What poverty, what weakness, what foolishness, I have been led into! how I have learned, in a sense, out of the reach of the comprehending, knowing mind; how tender I have been of every secret shining of light in my heart; how the Lord hath taught and enabled me to pluck out my right eye, and cut off my right hand, and cast them from me, that I might not see with that eye nor work with that hand, but be greatly maimed in the sight of men, and in my own sight too.

Oh, friend, wait daily to feel the seed, to feel the seed live in thee, and the most pleasing part of thy nature die, as it can live out of the seed. Oh that thou couldst change all old knowledge for that which is new and living! The seed is the well, receive the seed, then thou receivest the well: let it spring, wait for its springing, wait to know its springing: bear all the trials and judgments which the Father of life sees necessary to prepare the heart for its springing. Oh, feel that which limits and subdues thoughts and brings them into captivity and subjection! Be not exercised in things too high for thee;—David, the man after God's own heart, who was wiser than his teachers, was not;—but come out of knowledge into feeling, and there thou wilt find the true knowledge given,— arising, springing, and covering thy heart, as the waters cover the sea. And still wait to be taught of

God, to distinguish between the outwardness of knowledge,—the notional part of the thing known as it can be comprehended in the mind,—and the life of it, as it is felt and abides in the heart.

The Lord God of my life be thy Teacher; point thy mind to the pure seed of the kingdom, and open it in thee; make thee so little that thou mayst enter into it, and keep thee so low and poor that thou mayst abide in it; managing these troublesome times in the outward, for thy advantage in the inward; that the city and temple of the living God may be built in it, and thou mayst know him daily dwelling and walking therein. Thus mayst thou be married to the Lord, and become one spirit with him, finding that daily removing from thee, [which is to be removed, even] by the mighty arm and pure operation of his Spirit, till all that is contrary be done away; then, may thy soul dwell with its Beloved in fulness of joy, life, and peace for evermore!

This is from the tender love, and fresh breathings of life, in thy soul's true friend and most hearty well-wisher. I. P.

17th of Third Month, 1677.

## LETTER XXXI.

ON DISPUTATION, AND ON HEARING WISDOM'S VOICE—ALSO RESPECTING THE PURITAN STATE.

*To E. Terry.*

FRIEND:—

If the Lord hath extended favor to thee, and shown thee mercy, I therein rejoice on thy behalf.

Thy desire that what thou wrotest may be looked upon as nothing, and that no contest may be raised from it, I am content fully to answer thee in; nor do I desire to have any advantage against thee, nor art thou at all disparaged in my thoughts by what thou hast written, but it is in my heart as nothing, and my love flows to thee; for I take notice of thy seriousness, and what I have unity with in this letter, and overlook the other.

As touching disputes, indeed, I have no love to them: Truth did not enter my heart that way, nor do I expect to propagate it in others that way; yet sometimes a necessity is laid upon me for the sake of others. And truly, when I do feel a necessity I do it in great fear, not trusting in my spear or bow, I mean, in strong arguments or wise considerations, which I (of myself) can gather or comprehend; but I look up to the Lord for the guidance, help, and demonstration of his Spirit, that way may be made thereby in men's hearts for the pure seed to be reached to wherein the true conviction and thorough conversion of the soul to God is witnessed. I had far rather be feeling Christ's life, Spirit, and power in my own heart, than disputing with others about them.

Christians that truly fear the Lord have a proportion of the primitive Spirit; and, if they could learn to watch and wait there, where God works the fear, they would daily receive more and more of it, and, in it, understand more and more the true intent and preciousness of the words of the Holy Scriptures. He that will truly live to God must hear wisdom's voice within, at home, in his own heart; and he that will have her words made known, and her spirit poured out to him, must turn at her reproof. Prov. i. 23. Indeed, I never knew, and am satisfied that none else can know, the preciousness of this lesson till they are taught it of the Lord

There is one thing more on my heart to express, occasioned by thy last letter, which is this:—I have more unity in my heart and spirit before the Lord, with the Puritan state, than with the churches and gatherings which men have built up and run into since. Indeed, men have enlarged their knowledge and comprehension of things, but that truth of heart, that love, that tenderness, that unity upon Truth's account, which was then amongst them, many have made shipwreck of, and do not now know the state of their own souls, nor Truth in the life and power of it. This principle of life and truth was near me, as well as others; yea, with me in that day; but I wandered from it into outward knowledge, and with great seriousness, into a way of congregational worship, and thereby came to a great loss; and at length, for want of the Lord's presence, power, and manifestation of his love, was sick at heart. But now, the Lord, in great love and tender mercy, having brought me back to the same principle, and fixed my spirit therein, I discern the truth and beauty of that former estate, with the several runnings out from it; and find what was true or false therein discovered to me by the holy anointing which appears and teaches in that principle. And, friend, it is not a notion of light, which my heart is engaged to testify to; but that which enlivens, that which opens, that which gives to see, that wherein the power of life is felt. For truly, in the opening of my heart by the pure power was I taught to see and own the principle and seed of life, and to know its way of appearance; and so can faithfully and certainly testify that that which is divine, spiritual, and heavenly is nearer man than he is aware, as well as that which is earthly and selfish.

O friend! if thou canst not yet see and own the principle and seed of Christ's life and Spirit, nor discern his appearance therein, yet take heed of fighting against it, for indeed, if thou dost, thou fightest against no less than the Lord Jesus Christ himself.

I. P.

## LETTER XXXII.

ADVICE AS TO SELF-DECEIT—ON THE UNITY OF THE SPIRIT—THE YOUNGER ARE TO SUBMIT TO THE ELDER.

*To Miles Stanclif.*

Dear M. S.:—

Thou art often in my heart, and, indeed, I do many times bow unto the Father of Spirits for the preservation of whatever is good in thee, for the clear discovery to thee of what is not of his pure life, and for the separation of thy mind from it; that the life of Christ may conquer in thee, and thou thereby be fully redeemed to the Lord. I often inquire after thee, and, when I hear of any tenderness or diligence in thee towards the Truth, my heart rejoiceth therein.

Dear friend, deceit is very deep, and hath much prevailed, but the Lord is gathering out of it, and preparing such by the power of his life against future snares. Oh, dear friend! take heed of thy own wisdom, thy own sense, thy own judgment, which thou mayst easily, through mistake, call the Lord's: but to have all that is of self searched out and brought under, and the mind made truly sensible of, and fully subject to the life in every thing,—this is a sore travel; and it is very hard to come hither, through all deceits and entanglements. The Lord entirely join thy mind to that, and preserve thee in that which gives thee at any time a sense of Truth, and of those who are in the Truth: these are to be known and honored in the Lord according to their growth. And take heed of that which prejudices and disjoins; but feel and cleave to that which uniteth in love, life, and pure power. Know that unity and fellowship, which is in the Spirit; and keep it, keep it in the bond of pure peace, and take heed, oh, forever take heed, of whatever would break the bond! but that which makes of one mind and one judgment, one heart and one soul, *that* is the living principle, *that* is the living power which all the members of the body are to inhabit and be one in. And watch against the reasonings of the mind and the thoughts of thy heart; watch to the sense, which riseth up in the fear, in the love, in the humility, that thou mayst feel the leadings of God's Spirit, and come through all that stands in thy way; having the help of all whom the Lord hath ordained and made able to be helpers to thee. For life is not to be limited, but we are to be limited by that which is of the life; and, in cases of doubt, it is the ordinance of the Lord for the weak to receive counsel and help from the strong, and for the lesser to be watched over and blessed by the greater,—by such as are more grown in the life and into the power.

So, the Lord God Almighty lead thee fully into, and preserve thee perfectly in, the way everlasting!

Thy friend in the true love,         I. P.

16th of Third Month, 1668.

## LETTER XXXIII.

#### THE LOVING-KINDNESS OF THE LORD.

*To Elizabeth Walmsley, of Giles Chalfont.*

Dear Friend:—

The thoughts of thee are pleasant to me; indeed, I am melted with the sense of the Lord's love to thee as to my own soul.

What were we, that the Lord should stretch forth his arm to us, and gather us? And what are we, that the Lord should daily remember us in the issuings forth of his loving-kindness and mercies? Oh, his pity, his compassion, (must I forever say,) that my soul yet lives, and hath hope before him! And canst not thou also say the same? Oh, my friend! we feel mercy and salvation from the Lord. Oh that he might have pure praise and service from his own in us; and yet that will be little thanks to us, but rather a new mercy received from him. But all is his own, and of his own do we give him, and that only when he quickens, helps, and enables us to give. Dear friend, my desire for thee is, that the power and blessings of life may descend upon thee, and that thou mayst feel thy God near, and thy heart still ready to let him in and shut against all that is of a contrary nature to his; that thou mayst know *that* death passing upon thee, and perfected in thee, which prepares for, and lets into, the fulness of his pure, unspotted life.

Thou mayst commend my dear love to thy sister, and to all friends, as thou hast opportunity, who breathe after the Lord, and desire in uprightness of heart to walk with him.

I am thy friend in the affection which is of the Truth,                               I. P.

   AYLESBURY,
20th of Fourth Month, 1666.

## LETTER XXXIV.

### ON THE DANGER OF SELF-COMPLACENCY.

*To Catherine Pordage.*

FRIEND:—

In truth of heart and tender love to thee it is with me to return answers to the chief passages in thy letter as briefly as I may.

It hath not been my work to bring thee out of esteem or into esteem of persons. The Lord guide thee into true judgment and keep thee out of judging, except so far as that is raised in thee which the Lord maketh able to judge. But I have known several who have spoken most gloriously and ravishingly as to the Scriptures, opening things even to admiration, who have been out of the mystery of

Truth, and who have sparkled with the light and life of a wrong spirit, though they themselves knew it not to be so.

It is better with him who feels his unwillingness and waits to be made willing by the Lord, than with him who thinks he is willing, and, upon his own search, finds and judges himself to be so. I have thought I had been willing in several cases, and that if the Lord would have showed me his will I should have obeyed; which I found to be otherwise when the Lord came to lay the law of his Spirit and life upon me. This I am sure of; there is that in thee which is not willing to be impoverished, and I cannot say concerning thee, as in God's sight, that thou art yet separated from it. Now, while it is in thee it will be working in a mystery of deceivableness, hidden from thy heart, which thou canst not possibly discern but as the seed is raised, and the pure light shines in thee. Thou mayst easily think better of thyself than indeed it is with thee; but it is hard for thee in this thy present state to know what and how thou art in the sight of the Lord.

Thou shalt know the tenderness and melting compassion of the Lord when *that* is broken down in thee towards which his tenderness *is not*, and *that* raised up in thee and thy mind joined to it towards which his tenderness *is*; but great and subtle workings are there in thy mind from the enemy against God's truth, which thou dost not discern and eschew, but rather embrace, as if they were true and precious. If that tenderness were ministered to thee, either from God immediately, or from us, which thou expectest and desirest, (perhaps thinking thy state is wronged in not being so dealt with,) it might soon destroy thee, and that forever.

Thus, in great plainness have I written to thee, and beseech thee to be willing, or rather, to look up to the Lord to make thee willing, to have the wound kept open in thee, which the condition and state of thy soul needs; that it may be thoroughly searched, and that which is for judgment judged and destroyed; and so thy soul everlastingly saved by the everlasting Physician, who is wise and skilful in ministering both judgment and mercy to every one according to their need.

Thy friend in true, faithful, and unfeigned love and tenderness,          I. P.

25th of First Month, 1671.

---

## LETTER XXXV.

ACKNOWLEDGMENT OF CHRIST'S MANHOOD.

*To Richard Roberts.*

R. R. :—

Thou didst acquaint me that Timothy Fly, the Anabaptist teacher, did charge me with denying Christ's humanity, and also the blood of Christ, which was shed at Golgotha, without the gates of Jerusalem; and that I own no other Christ but what is within men.

Sure I am, that neither T. Fly, nor any other man, did ever hear me deny that Christ, according to the flesh, was born of the Virgin Mary, or that that was his blood which was shed without the gates of Jerusalem. And the Lord, who knoweth my heart, knoweth that such a thing never was in my heart; nay, I do greatly value that flesh and blood of our Lord Jesus Christ, and witness forgiveness of sins and redemption through it. Yet, if I should say I do not know nor partake of his flesh and blood in the mystery also, I should not be a faithful witness to the Lord. For there is the mystery of God and of Christ; and that is the soul's food which gives life to the soul, even the living bread and the living water. For there is living bread and living water; and the flesh and blood in the mystery on which the soul feeds is not inferior in nature and virtue to bread and water. There is a knowing Christ after the flesh, and there is a knowing him after the Spirit, and a feeding on his Spirit and life; and this doth not destroy his appearing in flesh, or the blessed ends thereof, but confirm and fulfil them.

The owning of Christ being inwardly in his saints doth not deny his appearing outwardly in the body prepared; unless T. F. can maintain this, that the same Christ that appeared outwardly cannot appear inwardly. "**Know ye** not your own selves, how that Jesus Christ is in you, except ye be reprobates?" 2 Cor. xiii. 5. "**And if** Christ be **in** you, the body is dead because of sin," &c. Rom. viii. **10.** "Christ in you, the hope of glory." Col. i. 27. "Behold, I stand at the door and **knock;** if any man hear my voice and open the **door, I** will come in to him." Rev. iii. 20. "**I will come again,**" saith Christ: Ye are now in pain, as a woman in travail, full of sorrow for the loss of my outward, bodily presence; **but I will come to you again in** spirit; see John xvi.; and John xiv. 16, "He," that "dwelleth with you, shall be in you:" and then, when the Bridegroom is inwardly and spiritually in you, and with you, "your heart shall rejoice, and your joy no man taketh from you." John xvi. **22.** And so the apostles and primitive Christians did "rejoice with joy unspeakable, and full of glory," 1 Peter i. 8, because **of the spiritual appearance and** presence of the Bridegroom. **And yet there is no other** bridegroom, who **now appears in spirit, or spiritually in the hearts of his, than He** that once **appeared** in the prepared body, and did the Father's will therein. I. P.

## LETTER XXXVI.

THE WAY TO LIFE NARROW—HARD THINGS MADE EASY TO THE OBEDIENT—ALSO, SOME ANSWERS TO OBJECTIONS ON PRAYER, ETC.

*To Catherine Pordage.*

FRIEND:—

It is true, the way to life is so difficult and intricate that none can find it but such as are lighted by the Lord and follow the guidance of his Spirit.

Christ, who preached the kingdom, and bid men seek it, yet said, "Strait is the gate and narrow is the way which leadeth unto life, and few there be that find it." In a race, many run, but one obtaineth the prize. Canst thou read what Christ said, "Except ye eat the flesh of the Son of man, and drink his blood, ye have no life in you;" that seemed a hard saying to some of his own disciples, many of whom left him. And truly, friend, as it is not an easy thing to come into the way, so neither is it an easy thing to abide in the way; for many are the by-paths, many and great the temptations, both on the right hand and on the left. The way was always the same, full as difficult and hard formerly as now; but the states and conditions of some make it harder to them than it is to others; yea, it is easier now than it hath been in many foregoing generations, being prepared and cast up by the Lord.

It is sad, indeed, that any should be convinced of Truth, and not come into subjection to it; yet it is very easy and common. For men cannot withstand conviction, when it comes in power; but they may deny obedience to that which they are convinced of; nay, some in the apostles' day went further, even to taste of the heavenly gift, and powers of the world to come, and to partake of the Holy Ghost, and yet fall away. Was not this very sad? and yet this was no well-grounded objection against the Truth and way of God then. Indeed, I make little of the illumination of the understanding, without subjection to Him that illuminateth, in those things wherein he illuminateth. But that is a great mistake, to suppose I did condemn any waiting or praying that is according to a true illumination and leading of God's Spirit; for the true light and spirit are not separated; but the exceptions I have against the prayers of professors is, that they are so much out of the true illumination, in a light of their own apprehending, forming, and conceiving. Now, these are but the limits of the fleshly birth, out of which comes nothing that is pleasing to the Father.

Did I, or any of us, ever affirm, that the forbearance of the means was the way to attain the end? But the setting up or using a false means is not the way to attain the true end. "So run," said the apostle, "that ye may obtain;" did he not forbid all running, but the right running? The praying of the fleshly birth, or in the will, and according to the wisdom of the flesh, is not the means or way to obtain the everlasting kingdom; but the prayers of the true birth are. And, if I should say thus again and again to thee, So pray, as that thou mayst obtain what thou prayest for, I should not be thine enemy therein; for it is easy asking amiss, not so easy to ask aright. Prayer is a gift; and he that receiveth it must first come to the sense of his own inability, and so wait to receive, and, perhaps, begin but with a groan or a sigh from the true Spirit, and thus grow in ability from the same Spirit, denying the ability which is after the flesh: this latter abounds in many, who mistake and err in judgment, not waiting on the Lord, to be enabled by him rightly to judge and distinguish between flesh and spirit, but are many times willingly ignorant in this particular, it will cost so dear to come to a true understanding therein.

Hath not all flesh had some manifestation of God's Spirit allotted it? was not that which might be known of God manifest in the Gentiles? and ought not all flesh, in that, to call upon the Lord, as the true sense is given them therefrom? But because of this, might the heathen pray according to their own imagination? Is there not a rule of prayer? Is not God's light, God's gift, God's Spirit, the rule to all? Is any prayer required or accepted out of this? Indeed, he that hath the sense of being but a dog, as I may say, and not worthy to be counted a child, yet may pray for crumbs, and be heard, and receive them. But what are prayers out of the light and life of God's Spirit? are they not prayers of the fleshly birth, fleshly will, fleshly wisdom? can they that are in the flesh, or pray in the flesh, please God? Oh forsake thy own wisdom, reasonings, will, and desires! that thou mayst come to true understanding in this particular.

As to stirring up the gift, 2 Tim. i. 6, Paul knew to whom he wrote: Timothy had a great understanding, and both knew the gift and how to stir it up; but he that hath not a true understanding may stir up somewhat else, instead of stirring up the gift, and so kindle a fire of his own, and offer up his own sacrifice, with his own fire, neither of which are acceptable to the Lord.

The troubled soul is not only to go to the Lord, but it must be taught by him, *how* to go to Him. The Lord is the Teacher; and *this* is a great lesson, which the soul cannot learn of itself, but as it is taught by him. Men abound in their several ways in religion, in that which God is arising to scatter and confound; so that it is not the great and main work to be found *doing*, but to be found doing *aright*, from the true teachings, and from the right Spirit.

In the time of great trouble, there may be life stirring underneath, and a true and tender sense, and pure desires, in which there may be a drawing nigh and breathing of heart to the Lord; but, in the time of trouble and great darkness, may not a man easily desire amiss, and pray amiss, if he have not his Guide? A little praying from God's Spirit, and in that which is true and pure, is better than thousands of vehement desires in one's own will, and after the flesh. For, as long as a man prayeth thus, that which should die in him lives in his very prayers; and how shall it ever be destroyed, if it get food and gain strength there? But, life and virtue may be felt, and that which troubleth be near too, and greatly troubling. Did Christ feel neither life nor virtue, in the time of his great trouble?

We neither lay weight on outward things, as considered in themselves, nor take off from the inward. Ah! consider what spirit this charge comes from; and if thou discern it, take heed of joining to it, and bringing forth the fruits of it any more. What if God hath chosen weak and foolish things to the eye of man's wisdom, now, as formerly? Do we, in so testifying, lay any more weight thereupon than God layeth? And what if God hath thrown by all preachings, prayings, singings, (yea, inward,) which are not in his Spirit, but from the transforming spirit and birth? Do we herein debase or testify against any thing that is inwardly of God? The *outward* which is right in God's sight must come from the *inward*, but not from the inward will or wisdom of the flesh, but from the inward light and Spirit of God; but it is a great matter to receive singly and go along with the inward light, and avoid the inward, deceitful appearance of things.

There is one thing hath been with me all along, still throughout thy letter, even a cry to thee for obedience, obedience to the Spirit and power of the Lord; and to consider whether disobedience hath not drawn this darkness and power of the enemy upon thee. It is not thy proper work to look out at the way, or think it hard, (for it is not so to the true seed,) but to be travelling in faithfulness, as thou art drawn and led; and this will save thee much sorrow.

As for Christ being a Mediator and Reconciler, it is by his death and life; both of which are partaken of, in the light which comes from him, even in the grace and truth which he dispenseth. For, as God wrought all in him by the fulness which he bestowed on him, so he works all in his by a measure of the same Spirit, life, and power. But why dost thou so desire to be able to comprehend and reason about these things? that is not thy present work, but to feel after and be joined to that whereby Christ reneweth and changeth the mind, and wherein he gives the knowledge of his good, and acceptable, and perfect will. Take heed of being exalted above measure, or desiring to know the things of the kingdom after the flesh; for it is better to lie low, and as a child to enter the kingdom, and to receive the knowledge of the things of God there, than to be feeding that knowing mind, which is to be kept out and famished.

Ah, watch, that thou mayst not lose thy Leader, and meet with the deceiver, instead of Him that is true; and so go back from light, life, truth, and power, instead of going forwards towards them. Indeed, this letter of thine makes me afraid, as Paul speaketh to the Galatians, lest I have bestowed labor on thee in vain; for there seems to me to be in thee a strengthening of thy mind towards returning back to that from which the Lord in his mercy hath been redeeming and gathering thee. If thou feel the right seed, and come to be of the right seed, the way of the seed will not be too hard for thee; otherwise, it will.

This is to thee, in love and grief, from thy soul's true friend, I. P.

21st of Sixth Month, 1671.

## LETTER XXXVII.

THE SCRIPTURES EXCEEDINGLY PRECIOUS—THE GOSPEL A MINISTRATION OF THE SPIRIT OF LIFE IN CHRIST JESUS—THE LIABILITY OF LOSING THE SENSE AND SAVOR OF THIS.

PROFESSORS have long known the name of Christ, and what the Scripture relateth concerning him so named; but oh that they could once know Christ [himself] and receive him into their vessels, and feel life flowing from him into them! Then would they indeed know Christ according to the Spirit; which knowledge quickeneth, but the literal knowledge killeth. For he that *hath* the Son, he that is in true union with him, and really changed by him, so as to become one nature and Spirit with him, *he* hath life; but he that hath not the Son hath not the life of the Son, nor the liberty of the Son, but it is in the death of sin, and in service unto sin.

The directions from God's Holy Spirit in the Scriptures are exceedingly weighty and precious in themselves, and very proper to the several states to which they were given forth; and blessed is he who is found in the practice and observation of them. And it hath been the desire of my heart from my childhood, and still is, that I might be found walking with the Lord, according to what is there taught and prescribed to the children of God, in the several foregoing ages and generations; which things were written and are useful for *our* instruction also, being read by us, and heeded in that which gives the true understanding of them.

But, though this was my desire, yet, in my way to attain this, I missed; for I thought that by getting the directions of Scripture into my mind, and applying myself to the strict observation of them, and praying for God's Spirit and help, I might obtain what I desired. And, truly, the Lord was merciful to me, and did help me, in a great measure, to walk uprightly and lowlily with him, and inoffensively before men; yet not so but that I often felt the temptations and darkness of the enemy nearer me than my rule, and in many cases knew not what to do, nor how to be resolved from the Scriptures.

At length the Lord greatly distressed me, and brought me to a fuller sense of my want of his

Spirit and power, and dashed all my religion in pieces; that I was just like Babylon, for in one hour judgment and desolation came upon me, Rev. xviii. 10; and I knew not what to do without the Lord, nor which way to draw nigh to him; but then was the Lord preparing for me that day of mercy which since, in his tender goodness, is broken in upon me. And now the eye which he hath opened in me seeth that the gospel is a ministration of the Spirit and power of the Lord Jesus Christ; and that he who would be his disciple indeed must be turned to his Spirit, and receive the immediate light and shinings of his Spirit into his vessel, and must feel the law of life, the holy laws of the new covenant, not comprehended outwardly in his mind, but written inwardly in his heart by the finger of God's Spirit. And, being written in his heart, they have power over his heart, and cause him to obey them; so that, being here, he cannot possibly but fulfil the holy directions of the Scriptures, he being in that from which they came, which reveals the substance of them unto him, and makes them living and powerful in him. For, indeed, the law of sin and death hath power over a man so long as he liveth; but, when he meets with that which kills sin and death in him, and maketh him alive to God, and he receives life in abundance in and through the Lord Jesus Christ; then the fruits of life become easy and natural to him, and the fruits and ways of sin, unbelief, and disobedience unnatural; and here the yoke is easy and the burden light, and none of the commandments of our Lord Jesus Christ grievous. But take them merely out of the letter, not feeling the Spirit leading into them, and quickening and enabling to the performance of them, oh, how heavy, how hard are they! How impossible to believe aright, hope aright, pray aright, walk aright, watch aright over the heart, fight against the enemies, lusts, and corruptions aright, &c. On the other hand, how pleasant is the way of life in the covenant of life, in the power and virtue of life, and ministered from the Spirit of our God! and here he is praised, and victory over his enemies witnessed, and peace with him enjoyed in the pure seed of life, blessed be the name of our God forever! For the letter or description of things is not the way; but the life is the way, the Spirit the way, the power the way, the truth as it is in Jesus the way, which none can truly and rightly know, but as they are ingrafted into and formed in him, and he formed in them; this is only obtained, witnessed, and preserved in the soul's union and communion with and obedience to his Spirit and power inwardly revealed and made manifest.

Friend, there is somewhat further in my heart towards thee, which I have the true and certain sense of, which is this: the Lord, who is near thee with his Holy Spirit and power, hath been begetting life in thee, and hath at times given thee a true sense and discerning, in some measure; but there is also somewhat near thee which watcheth to destroy and devour what the Holy Spirit of God begets in thee, and to beget another sense and belief in thee, different therefrom, and indeed contrary thereto. Now, it behoveth thee exceedingly to watch, and to pray to the Lord for help; for the life of thy soul depends upon the one of these, and death and destruction will inevitably break in upon thee, and have power over thee, if thou hearken to the other. Whom doth the enemy so much strive to devour as the sheep and inheritance of the Lord? And they are only preserved in the Lord's way, and in subjection to his Spirit. Oh, how many hath the enemy betrayed and deceived of the life of their souls! how many men's spirits are now cankered, and the good long ago eaten out of them, who had once some tenderness and upright breathings after the Lord; but now their silver is become dross, and their wine mixed with water, so that the very nature and property of it is changed; the salt having lost its savor, wherewith shall it be seasoned? I mention this to thee, that thou mayest watch and pray; that thou thyself do not lose thy savor, and sense, and tenderness, which the Lord at some times kindleth in thee, by hearkening to the subtle reasonings and suggestions of another spirit, either in thyself or others.

This is in the nakedness of my heart, as in the Lord's sight, and in the truth of friendship towards thee. I. P.

27th of Ninth Month, 1670.

## LETTER XXXVIII.

THE UNSEARCHABLE RICHES OF CHRIST—BELIEVERS MAY PARTAKE THEREOF THROUGH OBEDIENCE, AND BE PRESERVED FROM EVERY HARM.

*To Friends of both the Chalfonts.*

Oh, the treasures of wisdom and knowledge, the riches of love, mercy, life, power, and grace of our God which are treasured up for the soul in the Lord Jesus, and are freely dispensed and given out by him to them that come unto him, wait upon him, abide in him, and give up faithfully to the law of his life; whose delight it is to be found in subjection and obedience to the light and requirings of his Spirit.

Feel, my friends, oh, feel your portion, and abide in that wherein the inheritance is known, received, and enjoyed. For there is no knowing Christ truly and sensibly but by a measure of his life felt in the heart, whereby it is made capable of understanding the things of the kingdom. The soul without him is dead: by the quickenings of his Spirit it comes to a sense and capacity of understanding the things of God. Life gives it a feeling, a sight, a tasting, a hearing, a smelling of the heavenly things, by which senses it is able to discern and distinguish them from the earthly things. And from this measure of life the capacity increaseth, the senses grow stronger; it sees more, feels more, tastes more, hears more, smells more. Now, when the senses are grown up to strength, then comes settlement and stability, assurance and satisfaction. Then the soul is assured of and established concerning the things of God in the faith, and the faith gives assurance to the understanding, so that doubtings and disputes in the mind fly away, and the soul lives in the certain demonstration, and fresh sense and power of life. It daily feels the eternal Word and power of life to be, in the heart and soul, what is testified of it in the Scripture. It knows the flesh and blood of the Lamb, the water and wine of the kingdom, the bread which comes down from heaven into the vessel, from all other things, by its daily feeding on it, and converse with it in spirit. What heart can conceive the righteousness, the holiness, the peace, the joy, the strength of life that is felt here!

For, friends, there is no straitness in the Fountain. God is fulness; and it is his delight to empty himself into the hearts of his children; and he doth empty himself according as he makes way in them, and as they are able to drink in of his living virtue. Therefore, where the soul is enlarged, where the senses are grown strong, where the mouth is opened wide, (the Lord God standing ready to pour out of his riches,) what should hinder it from being filled? And, being filled, how natural is it to run over, and break forth inwardly in admiration and deep sense of spirit concerning what it cannot utter, saying, Oh, the fulness, oh, the depth, height, breadth, and length of the love! oh, the compassion, the mercy, the tenderness of our Father! How hath he pitied, how hath he pardoned beyond what the heart could believe; how hath he helped in the hour of distress; how hath he conquered and scattered the enemies, which, in the unbelief, the heart was ready often to say were unconquerable, and that it should one day die by the hand of one or other of its mighty enemies, lusts, and corruptions. How hath he put an end to doubts, fears, disputes, troubles, wherewith the mind was overwhelmed and tossed; and now he extends peace like a river; now he puts the soul forth out of the pit into the green pastures; now it feeds on the freshness of life and is satisfied, and drinks of the river of God's pleasure and is delighted, and sings praise to the Lamb, and Him that sits on the throne, saying, Glory, glory! life, power, dominion, and majesty, over all the powers of darkness, over all the enemies of the soul, be to thy name for evermore!

Now, my dear friends, ye know somewhat of this, and ye know the way of it. Oh, be faithful, be faithful! travel on, travel on; let nothing stop you; but wait for and daily follow the sensible leadings of that measure of life which God hath placed in you, which is one with the fulness, and into which the fulness runs daily and fills it that it may run into you and fill you. Oh that ye were enlarged in your own hearts, as the bowels of the Lord are enlarged towards you! It is the day of love, of mercy, of kindness, of the working of the tender hand, of the wisdom, power, and goodness of our God, manifested richly in Jesus Christ! Oh, why should there be any stop in any of us? The Lord remove that which stands in the way; and in the faithful waiting on the power which is arisen the Lord doth remove, yea, the Lord doth remove; and growth in his truth and power is witnessed by those that wait upon him. So, my dear friends, be encouraged to wait upon the Lord in the pure fear, in the precious faith and hope which is of him; and ye will see and feel; he will exalt the horn of his Anointed in you over the horn of that which is unanointed, and will sweep, and cleanse, and purify, even till he hath left no place for the impure: and then ye shall become his full dwelling-place, the place of his rest, the place of his delight, the place of his displaying his pure life and glory; and he will be your perfect dwelling-place for evermore!

May the Lord God in his tender mercy, and because of his deep and free love unto us, guide our hearts daily more and more in the travel, and into the possession of this; that every soul may inherit and possess, notwithstanding all its enemies, what it hath travelled into, and may also daily further and further travel into what is yet before. I. P.

AYLESBURY JAIL,
2d and 3d of Sixth Month, 1667.

## POSTSCRIPT.

Friends:—

Be not discouraged because of your soul's enemies. Are ye troubled with thoughts, fears, doubts, imaginations, reasonings, &c.? yea, do ye see yet much in you unsubdued to the power of life? Oh, do not fear it; do not look at it so as to be discouraged by it; but look to Him; look up to the power which is over all their strength; wait for the descendings of the power upon you; abide in faith of the Lord's help, and wait in patience till the Lord arise, and see if his arm do not scatter what yours could not. So be still before him, and in stillness believe in his name; yea, enter not into the hurryings of the enemy, though they fill the soul; for there is somewhat to which they cannot enter, from whence patience, faith, and hope will spring up in you, even in the midst of all that they can do.

Therefore, into *this* sink; in *this* lie hid in the evil hour, and the temptations will pass away, and the tempter's strength be broken, and the arm of the Lord, which brake him, be revealed; and then ye shall see that he raised but a sea of trouble to your souls to sink himself by; and the Lord will throw the horse and his rider, which trampled upon and rode over the just in you, into that sea; and ye shall stand upon the bank and sing the song of Moses to Him that drowned him, and delivered you from him; and in due season ye shall sing the song of the Lamb also.

when his life springs up in you in his pure dominion, triumphing over death, and all that is contrary to God both within and without.

Now, friends, in a sensible waiting and giving up to the Lord in the daily exercise, by the daily cross to that in you which is not of the life, this work will daily go on, and ye will feel from the Lord that which will help, relieve, refresh, and satisfy; which neither tongue nor words can utter. And may the Lord God breathe upon you, preserve and fill you with his life and Holy Spirit, to the growth and rejoicing of your souls in Him who is our blessed Father and merciful Redeemer; in the Lord Jesus Christ, our Head and King forever and for evermore!

And then as to what may befall us outwardly in this confused state of things, shall we not trust our tender Father, and rest satisfied in his will? Are we not engraven in his heart, and on the palms of his hands, and can he forget us in any thing he doth? Shall any thing hurt us? Shall any thing come between us and our life, between us and his love, and tender care over us? What though the figtree should not blossom, neither there be any fruit in the vine; what though the labor of the olive should fail, and the fields yield no meat; what though the flock be cut off from the fold, and there be no herd in the stalls; may we not, for all this, rejoice in the Lord, and joy in the God of our salvation? And what though the earth be removed, and the mountains carried into the midst of the sea; what though the waters thereof roar and be troubled, and the mountains shake with the swelling thereof; is there not a river, the streams whereof make glad the city of God? Is not the joy, the virtue, the life, the sweet refreshment thereof, felt in the holy place of the tabernacle of the Most High? And He that provides inward food for the inward man, inward clothing, inward refreshment, shall he not provide also sufficient for the outward? Yea, shall he not bear up the mind, and be our strength, portion, armor, rock, peace, joy, and full satisfaction in every condition? For it is not the condition makes miserable, but the want of him in the condition: he is the substance of all, the virtue of all, the life of all, the power of all; he nourisheth, he preserveth, he upholdeth, with the creatures or without the creatures, as it pleaseth him; and he that hath him, he that is with him, he that is in him, cannot want. Hath the spirit of this world content in all that it enjoys? No: it is restless, it is unsatisfied. But can tribulation, distress, persecution, famine, nakedness, peril, or sword, come between the love of the Father to the child, or the child's rest, content, and delight in his love? And doth not the love, the peace, the joy, the rest felt, swallow up all the bitterness and sorrow of the outward condition?

The seed, the godliness, the uprightness, the true nature and birth, hath not only the promise of eternal life; but also whatever is necessary for the vessel wherein it dwells in this life too. So dwell in that to which is the promise, and live upon the promise; yea, live upon that which cannot miss of the promise, but feels the presence and power of the Father in all and over all. The just lives by his faith; and he that is in union with the just lives by the faith of the just, and takes no more care than the lilies, but leaves the care of all to Him to whom it properly belongs, and who hath taken it upon him; who nourishes, clothes, preserves, and causes the lilies of the field to grow and flourish in beauty and glory: and shall he not much more clothe, nourish, and take care of his own lilies, the heavenly lilies, the lilies of his garden?

Let us, then, not look out like the world, or judge or fear according to the appearance of things after the manner of the world; but let us sanctify the Lord of hosts in our hearts, and let him be our fear and dread; and he shall be an hiding-place unto us in the storms, and in the tempests, which are coming thick upon the earth.

Thus, my dear friends, let us retire and dwell in the peace which God breathes, and lie down in the Lamb's patience and stillness, night and day, which nothing can wear out or disturb; and so the preservation of the poor and needy shall be felt to be in his name; and glory shall be sung to his name over all, which is a strong tower, a mighty, impregnable rock of defence against all assaults and dangers whatsoever; which they that have trusted therein have already experienced it to be; and they that continue trusting therein shall always experience it so to be in all trials and dangers, whatever may happen, of what kind soever, even to the end. Amen.

## LETTER XXXIX.

### FAITHFUL DEALING BETWEEN BRETHREN RECOMMENDED.

Dear Friend:—

I have heard that thou hast somewhat against W. R., whereupon thou forbearest coming to meetings at his house: this thou oughtst seriously to weigh and consider, that thy path and walking herein may be right and straight before the Lord. Is the thing or are the things which thou hast against him fully so as thou apprehendest? Hast thou seen evil in him, or to break forth from him? and hast thou considered *him* therein, and dealt with him as if it had been thy own case? Hast thou pitied him, mourned over him, cried to the Lord for him, and, in tender love and meekness of spirit, laid the thing before him? And if he hath refused to hear thee, hast thou tenderly mentioned it to others, and desired them to go with thee to him, that what is evil and offensive in him might be more weightily and advantageously laid before him for his humbling, and for his recovery into that which is a witness and strength against the evil? If thou hast proceeded thus, thou hast proceeded tenderly and orderly, according to the law of brotherly love, and God's witness in thy conscience will justify thee therein. But if thou hast let in any hardness of spirit or hard reasonings against him, or hard resolutions as relating to him, the witness of God will not justify thee in that.

And if at any time hereafter thou hast any thing against others, oh, learn from that of God in thee to show compassion towards them, even as the Lord has had pity on thee! And keep to his witness in thy heart; wait to feel the seed, and to keep thy dwelling therein, that thou mayst abide in the peace and rest thereof, and not depart out of thy habitation, out of the sense of Truth; for that will let in temptation upon thee, give the enemy strength against thee, and fill thy soul with anguish and perplexity.

So, the Lord God of infinite tenderness renew his mercy upon thee, and keep thee in that wherein his love, life, rest, joy, peace, and unspeakable comfort of his Holy Spirit, (which keeps the mind out of all the snares and temptations of that which is unholy,) is felt and witnessed by those who are taught and enabled of him to abide and dwell in that into which he hath gathered them, and in which he hath pleased to appear unto them.

This is, in the love and tender goodness of the Lord, to thee, from thy friend in the Truth and for the Truth's sake. I. P.

13th of Tenth Month, 1667.

www.ingramcontent.com/pod-product-compliance
Lightning Source LLC
Chambersburg PA
CBHW022139160426
43197CB00009B/1352